Never Threaten to Eat Your Co-Workers: Best of Blogs

EDITED BY ALAN GRAHAM AND BONNIE BURTON

Apress™

Never Threaten to Eat Your Co-Workers: Best of Blogs

Project Manager: Tracy Brown Collins

Copy Manager: Nicole LeClerc

Copy Editor: Nancy Depper

Production Manager: Kari Brooks

Production Editor: Laura Cheu

Compositor: Susan Glinert

Proofreader: Linda Seifert

Artist: John Burton

Cover Designer: John Burton, Kurt Krames

Manufacturing Manager: Tom Debolski

Library of Congress Cataloging-in-Publication Data

Never threaten to eat your co-workers : best of blogs / Edited by Alan Graham and Bonnie Burton.

p. cm.

Includes bibliographical references and index.

ISBN 1-59059-321-9

I. Graham, Alan, 1971- II. Burton, Bonnie, 1972-

AC8.N474 2004

081--dc22

2004004814

Printed and bound in the United States of America 10987654321

Distributed to the book trade in the United States by Springer-Verlag New York, Inc., 175 Fifth Avenue, New York, NY 10010 and outside the United States by Springer-Verlag GmbH & Co. KG, Tiergartenstr. 17, 69112 Heidelberg, Germany.

In the United States: phone 1-800-SPRINGER, e-mail orders@springer-ny.com, or visit http://www.springer-ny.com. Outside the United States: fax +49 6221 345229, e-mail orders@springer.de, or visit http://www.springer.de.

For information on translations, please contact Apress directly at 2560 Ninth Street, Suite 219, Berkeley, CA 94710. Phone 510-549-5930, fax 510-549-5939, e-mail info@apress.com, or visit http://www.apress.com.

Alan Graham dedicates this book to his wife Dana, his daughter Emry, and his good friends Nick Sholley and John Forté.

Free John Forté

http://carlysimon.com/forte/John_Forte.html

Contents

Foreword

I'm a techblogger. Half or more of what I write is about technology. Mostly it's tech stuff outside the scope of my day job as Senior Editor for *Linux Journal*. Some of it is about blogging itself. Some of it is about old technology-based media like radio, TV, and publishing, which I've been around since the turn of the Seventies.

A lot of what I write is about journalism, which I am pleased to see reequipped and transformed by weblog technologies. By transforming millions of passive users into active journalists, blog tech is equipping the Huns to overrun Rome. It's a wonderful thing to watch. I hated Rome.

Amazingly, Big-J journalism hardly knows it's being sacked and taken over by all these little-j journalist because Big-J media, on the whole, hardly know what to make of the Web that's been around since 1995, much less of the latest developments there. So they trivialize blogging and dismiss it as "noise." I still haven't seen a good major media story about blogging that isn't by a blogger.

Even my favorite broadcast journalist, Scott Simon of NPR, had an essay on blogging last November that was wrong and dumb from start to finish. In the absence of knowledge he offered nothing but dismissive prejudice. It was disappointing but understandable. He's a Roman, doing what the Romans do.

It's not all the Romans' fault. Blogs can't be understood, much less explained, in terms of the conceptual metaphors we've used to describe the Web since its beginning: all that stuff about "designing," "putting up," "building," and "constructing" Web "sites" with "addresses" and "locations." There's nothing in the borrowed rhetoric of architecture, construction, and real estate that can begin to describe what Dave Winer, Glenn Reynolds, and Choire Sicha do with their blogs every day.

They crush statues with every sentence they write. They also enlarge the tapestry of civilization with every link they make, every thread they weave.

They do it by speaking in their own voices about the subjects that interest them, regardless of whatever categories others might like to impose.

They do both by reporting news faster, more accurately, and often less conclusively than what you'll read in the papers, hear on the radio or watch on TV.

Thanks to hypertext, the Web is not only a medium for writing, but for rewriting. It's perfectly suited for what Jefferson called "the fugitive fermentation of an individual brain."

Hypertext lets us move and connect our ideas in ways that transcend our individual interests. Thus the best medium ever invented for personal expression is also the best for demonstrating what Jefferson was talking about in his letter to Isaac McPherson in 1813:

> *If nature has made any one thing less susceptible than all others of exclusive property, it is the action of the thinking power called an idea, which an individual may exclusively possess as long as he keeps it to himself; but the moment it is divulged, it forces itself into the possession of every one, and the receiver cannot dispossess himself of it. Its peculiar character, too, is that no one possesses the less, because every other possesses the whole of it. He who receives an idea from me, receives instruction himself without lessening mine; as he who lights his taper at mine, receives light without darkening me. That ideas should freely spread from one to another over the globe, for the moral and mutual instruction of man, and improvement of his condition, seems to have been peculiarly and benevolently designed by nature, when she made them, like fire, expansible over all space, without lessening their density in any point, and like the air in which we breathe, move, and have our physical being, incapable of confinement or exclusive appropriation. Inventions then cannot, in nature, be a subject of property.*

I began writing about hypertext's subversion of big-J journalism long before I started blogging in 1999. But I didn't even think about the simultaneous subversion of big-L literature until Alan Graham sent me the selections gathered for this book. I realized for the first time that bloggers are also producing real literature at a prodigious rate, and in immeasurable quantities, all of it equally personal and connected, all of it unbent by a publisher's agenda.

When I read this new literature, I finally hear fulfilled the muscular commands and prophesies issued by Walt Whitman in "Song of Myself":

You shall no longer take things at second or third hand...

nor look through the eyes of the dead,

nor feed on the spectres in books.

You shall not look through my eyes either,

nor take things from me.

You shall listen to all sides and filter them for yourself...

...

Long enough have you dreamed contemptible dreams.

Now I wash the gum from your eyes.

You must habit yourself to the dazzle of the light and of every moment of your life.

Long have you timidly waited,

holding a plank by the shore.

Now I will you to be a bold swimmer,

To jump off in the midst of the sea, and rise again,

and nod to me and shout,

and laughingly dash your hair.

I am the teacher of athletes.

He that by me spreads a wider breast than my own

proves the width of my own.

He most honors my style

who learns under it to destroy the teacher.[1]

In late 1998, Chris Locke and I found ourselves in long conversations about how wrongly the Internet was understood by just about everybody

1. http://searls.com/whitman.html

who opined about it in Major Media. We were just as flummoxed by watching huge quantities of dumb money funding doomed business ideas based on the same wrong ideas—for example, that Web sites were about "capturing eyeballs" and holding them still while banner ads "penetrated" them with advertising messages. Or that the Web's real estate was best suited for the online equivalent of suburban shopping malls.

At one point I shared with Chris the logic behind my philosophy of marketing:

Markets are conversations; and

Conversation is fire. Therefore,

Marketing is arson.

Chris said "Let's test that theory." He had been having related conversations with David Weinberger on the same subjects; so the three of us got together, recruited technologist Rick Levine and produced *The Cluetrain Manifesto* (`http://www.cluetrain.com`): ninety-five "theses" we hoped might be as combustible on the Web in 1999 as Martin Luther's were when he nailed them to a church door in 1517.

Cluetrain caught fire. A few days after it went up in late March, the buzz reached *The Wall Street Journal*, where Tom Petzinger wrote a column about it. Within a few more days we had a book deal, and by the end of the summer we had a finished draft. The book came out in January 2000 (the same month the dot-com crash began) and immediately became a nonfiction bestseller.

Cluetrain still sells well, in nine languages. Today (in mid-December 2003) its Amazon sales rank is 822, out of millions. A few days ago I got the latest Chinese edition in the mail.

I can't prove it, but I'm sure Cluetrain's continued success is due at least in part to its authors' weblogs, and others influenced by them. Those include democratic presidential candidate Howard Dean, whose chief Internet advisor is David Weinberger.

Whether you want to set fire to old institutions or to build whole new ones, nothing beats a good blog.

Doc Searls

Co-Author, *The Cluetrain Manifesto*

About the Editors

Alan Graham is the creator and editor of the Best of Blogs series. A digital chameleon, his career in technology spans over 10 years; he has worked with some of the biggest and brightest companies in the Internet firmament. During that time, appearances include *Wired* magazine, *The London Observer*, Po Bronson's *The Nudist on the Lateshift* (sadly, he is not the nudist), and the Jim Lehrer NewsHour. Since leaving the business side of technology for a writing career three years ago, he has become an author for O'Reilly & Associates, Apress, and WordWare, and he has written for *MacWorld* magazine, *MacAddict* magazine, and the *O'Reilly Network*. Most notably, Alan planned and executed a trip sponsored by CompUSA and Handspring to traverse 10,000 miles, through 20+ states, in just 30 days, using only his trusty PDA to navigate and document the trip. He plans a second trip later this year. His regular columns and blog can be found on the O'Reilly Network at: `http://www.oreillynet.com/pub/au/165`.

Bonnie Burton submersed herself into Web culture long before the word "blogging" was even coined. She's written about everything from online dating adventures to unusual eBay.com collecting obsessions. Her work has appeared in the magazines *Wired, The Net, Yahoo Internet Life, BUST,* and *Organic Gardening* as well as online at @Home Network, MissClick.com, Backwash.com, Winamp.com, and Teenwire.com. She has appeared as a Web pop culture media expert on E! Television, CNN Headline News, BBC, ABC News, Tokyo Broadcasting System and TechTV; and she has been featured in the books: *Complete Idiot's Guide to Online Dating and Relating, Net Chick, Fierce.Com, Alt.Culture: An A-To-Z Guide to the '90s-Underground, Online, Over-The-Counter,* and *The Real Bettie Page.* The Bonnie Blog and additional columns can be found on her Web site, Grrl.com.

About the Artist

John Burton is a graphic designer and freelance illustrator living in Connecticut. His recent projects include illustrations for Teenwire.com, Grrl.com, and various other pop culture Web sites. To see more of his illustrations, bizarre haiku, and unfinished plays, visit his Web site, Ragingsquirrel.com.

Acknowledgments

Alan Graham would like to thank Bonnie Burton for her tireless work. Thanks to Martin Streicher for recognizing a good idea and helping to make it a reality. And finally, thanks to all of the bloggers in the book and the blogging community. Your enthusiastic support during this book kept me going. Without you, these pages would be empty. Here's to a new era in publishing!

Bonnie Burton thanks: my mom who always encouraged me to write, my dad for teaching me to set goals, and all my friends and fellow bloggers who filled me with inspiration, encouragement, and strawberry Pocky.

Introduction

Weblog (blog)—A journaled web site composed of personal observations, often with excerpts from additional web sites. Blogs are sometimes associated with online journals or diaries, but are quickly evolving to encompass and suit the needs of their authors.

A year and a half ago...in the middle of a particularly steamy brainstorming session, somewhere between the Calvin Klein bar soap and the loofa, I was struck with an idea. I was reflecting on an excellent weblog (blog) entry and the remarkable evolution and emergence of the blog in our daily lives, I thought to myself that a lot of this content was as good as anything in print today. I had come to the realization that blogging was not only redefining journalism, but was quickly revolutionizing literature as well. I noticed that I was starting to read more online blog content and less content from magazines and other literary sources.

As a writer, my own blogging is an exercise in saying more with less, and the art of self-editing, a tool to help me be a better writer. But what I found remarkable is that thousands, if not millions, of bloggers aren't professional writers. They push brooms, cook food, park cars, clean hotel rooms, etc. There was this entire writing community who never perceived of themselves as writers, they just had something to say.

Some of it was funny, some thought provoking, but regardless of the message, the one constant is that each blog gives us an in-depth view of another person, without the message being clouded by an editor. Millions of daily observations, thoughts, experiences, memories, rants, all condensed into these neatly packed moments across the World Wide Web.

As I toweled off I thought to myself, these people deserve to be published and discovered by others. And so began the journey that would later become this book series.

However...

I found that reading blogs, and more importantly, finding good content, was complicated and time consuming. I was looking for a few needles in an ever-expanding haystack. Together with my co-editor, Bonnie Burton, we spent months reading and collecting the best content we could find. We then struggled for months on how to best present the material. Nothing like this had ever been done before, so no guidelines existed.

Now, some purists will say that translating the blog into print defies everything the blog stands for. It loses some of its power and impact. It loses the dynamic link that makes it a living thing. But, I'd say to them that ideas are always living things, regardless of the medium, because they are linked between our minds. Great ideas transcend their medium and what we found were great ideas.

This book has no political agenda. The task was simply to find people who knew how to convey their thoughts in a way that might make you think, challenge your views, make you laugh or cry, and possibly inspire you to add your voice to theirs. We wanted to be the *Consumer Reports* of blogging.

So enjoy!

How to Use This Book

Other than the obvious act of reading, you might be interested in how to get the most out of this book.

In order to preserve the feel that what you are reading is literature, we've placed all the information about each blog (site name and URL) at the end of each entry. In addition, you'll find an index in the back of the book so you can easily locate entries from a particular blogger.

Finally, since the only permanent thing you can count on is change, in the event that an author might remove or move their site to a new home on the web, we've assembled a web site to keep this information timely:

`http://bestblogs.blogdns.com`

Also on this web site, you'll find links to a number of bloggers who unfortunately didn't make the final cut of the book. Due to the inevitable issue of page count restrictions, we had to leave out some of our favorite bloggers. So if you enjoy the book and want to take a spin around what we also thought were remarkable entries, please visit the site. And just in case you feel inspired, we've also included a guide with information to help you too get started blogging.

On page 251 you'll find the Editor FAQ which contains all the information on how we assembled this book. Since every aspect of the project was something that hadn't been done before, the learning curve was challenging. And we're still learning. In fact, I want to hear from you. If you want to see us change something, have a suggestion, or just want to give some feedback, you can personally email me at `agraham999@mac.com`. Like the bloggers in this book, you are part of this project and your input matters.

Thank you for purchasing this book. Each of the blogging contributors is paid an equal percentage of royalties. Your purchase is a show of support for the blogging community and for a new type of literature. It will also help to ensure other Best of Blog books in the future.

Alan Graham

Editor

Bling Bling Strategies For The New Economy

Choire Sicha

I spent all day in the land that money forgot: Manhattan's criminal court. For my dreary day of co-mingling with the poor on jury duty, I chose to blend in, with my hair down and clad only in a simple outfit of jeans and a wifebeater. While crammed ass to elbow in the stuffy courts with the personal trainers and social workers and school teachers and of course criminals, I thought: of course I'm not like these impecunious people. But what does really differentiate me from them—besides goals, taste, and lifestyle? The most important gulf between us should really be money itself.

And it isn't. I don't actually have any money. Sure, it's all cabs, delivery, Prada, beach house, Schwab accounts, and Soho House with me. Sure, my acupuncturist messengered me a bag of vitamins last week. And of course I chainsmoke, the last sign of wealth in these unhedonist times. But these cigarettes are from Switzerland! Two dollars a pack! Like a transsexual supermodel at Beige, I'm a fraud where it counts the most.

As the judge prattled on in court this afternoon, I stopped thinking about the state of my dot-com savaged brokerage account long enough to consider the fate of the defendant on trial—just long enough, that is, to say something objectionable (and quite truthful) enough to get me thrown out of the jury box. Then I put my mind to work on my finances, and I've come up with a splendid idea.

Many of you have too much money and real estate and not enough good times and able assistance. It seems that I am in a perfect position to assist in this imbalance. I can provide this special class, the Lonely Wealthy, with services heretofore undreamt of.

Just for instance: having recently seen first-hand how slowly and improperly the wheels of justice actually turn, I am willing and able to provide sub-legal services for the rich. Once upon a time in bygone New York there was a job title of "The Heavy." The Heavy would collect debts, run errands, and ensure that income streams remained undroughted. As a shadowy and fagulous denizen of Lower Manhattan, I am nonplussed by the breaking of pinkie fingers. I am an excellent shot with a pearl-handled .22, and I am licensed to carry teargas in the great state of California. Violence is certainly one common ground where my interests could converge with those of the rich.

I know also that the rich are often surrounded by toadies and yes-people. Being a homosexual and a total bastard, and therefore completely unimpressed by your celebrity, I am willing to tell you about your hideous wigs, bad shoes, slutty wife, and stupid stock sales. Here's how it works: I lounge about in your home office or yacht galley. Everytime I say something cruel yet honest to you, you throw a twenty dollar bill at me. You supply the cocktails, I bring the loving truth.

Best of all, my grand scheme is for an afterlife aftercare program. Perhaps, like so many of the wealthy, you are very old, and you may die soon. Like all rich people, you certainly have vendettas and evil schemes. Utilizing utmost discretion, you may exercise attorney-client privilege as you draw up your will, secretly hiring me without my—or anyone else's—previous knowledge. Pay what you feel the service is worth, but I'll give some possible sample rates and missions:

- I can promise that your widow is blacklisted from Patrick McMullan's benefit circuit party pictures in *New York Magazine* and *Interview* by constantly posing with her: 15 grand yearly plus cost of benefit tickets (and tuxedo cleaning, if you're feeling charitable).

- I can throw a giant grieving homosexual hissy fit at your funeral, with guaranteed *New York Post* coverage, forever traumatizing your spouse and/or lover(s) and guaranteeing your place in the grand pantheon of sexually enigmatic powerbrokers: 8 grand.

- Ungrateful children special: no money down! Merely leave your properties jointly to both me and whichever child deserves constant painful remembrance of you. Please leave me a specific video last will and testament demonstrating your choice of nagging and shaming techniques. Your only payment will be the real estate you already own—it's like it's free!

Other ideas to consider:

- appoint me to the board of a family foundation or independent corporation to do your vicious yet deceased financial maneuvering, or,
- leave me your servants in your will; I will take them in and make them scour my East Village sideboards and alphabetize my CDs endlessly, or,
- have me installed on a local community board or parks conservancy to undermine the environment and overdevelop neighborhoods from beyond the grave, or...
- have you ever been annoyed by other meddlesome rich people? Perhaps you'd like to have your revenge from the Other Side and never get fingered. I will t.p. houses, stinkbomb board rooms, egg limousines, and stalk nearly anyone, for a very very low price, or perhaps if you're more interested in global disruption you could...
- purchase me an ambassadorship to a banana republic where I may exploit coca bean growers and encourage "international trade,"

and oh so very much more. You got yourself rich, so be a little creative. In short, having seen what happens to the poor up close and personal, I will kill, maim, butcher, harass, plague, and have sex with anyone for the right price. Your wish is my command; wire transfer operators are standing by.

Site: Choire Sicha Dot Com

URL: http://choiresicha.com

Why George F. Will?

Jeff Dorchen

Hello and welcome to the Moment of Truth, the owl at the pet store you should have bought and taken home with you because now you and your nation of helpless ankles are plagued by the nipping of a sea of rats.

There is one question in my mind: Why George Will? Why? Why is there a George Will? Why is George Will George Will? And why is George Will George Will in the particularly George Willian way he is?

It's too simple to say that George Will is a rightwing columnist who appears every other week or so on the back page of Newsweek. The truth is much deeper. George Will, or George F. Will as he is usually bylined, is more like a stifled human spirit clapped up in the bony prison of an irritated-looking head, choked off at the base by a bowtie that dares you to stoop to the pettiness of mocking it. This knob of despair sits atop a metaphorical robot of the mindless insect-like variety and has been set down in a maze of rightwing semiotics where it scurries from obstacle to passageway as if with will and purpose. But it possesses neither will nor the coherence of action a will might bestow. Hence, I suppose, the F. before the surname Will. "F. will," George Will's career seems to say. "F. coherence and F. will."

He begins one of his recent columns thus: "As if it was not already as plain as a pikestaff..." And who cares what comes after that? It's the bowtie challenge all over again. Will seems to dare us to mock his pikestaff, to mock his diction, yet at the same time he's daring us to continue reading with any measure of calm intellectual detachment. Because who can pay attention to what this shmuck is talking about when he's stuck this big clunky bizarre psychotic PIKESTAFF into the beginning of his column? Pikestaff? Plain as a pikestaff? What do you even know about plain if your first example is a pikestaff? And yet there you are, with your challenging bowtie, saying pikestaff. And all with a straight face. And after all you did edit the National Review. I guess after that you can just wave pikestaffs and bowties around like there'll be no consequences whatsoever. Are you mad, George Will? Or are you crazy like a fox?

Then get this, three brief sentences in: "...Wesley Clark, the retired Army general who fancies himself a president, has suddenly discovered, in his 59th year, that he is a Democrat."

Just listen to that contempt. I know it's hard to focus on with the pursed lips and the bowtie and pikestaff. But that is some serious contempt there. Fancies himself a president. Oh, does he? Fancy himself a president, does he? Fancy himself a poet, does he, our little Mr. Floyd? And our Mr. Fredrick Douglass, does this darkie actually fancy himself an orator? And does this poor ragged tailor fancy he can win the hand of the lovely Princess Pendragon?

The reader has been transported in the space of a few lines of prose into an unfamiliar and terrifying universe. It's a vision more disorienting than that painted by John Lennon in "Lucy in the Sky with Diamonds"; there we had newspaper taxis and cellophane flowers, but at least everyone was smiling. There's something almost reassuring about the plasticine porters' looking glass ties when compared with the dour bowtie of our Mr. Will. And that pikestaff of his. Good lord! He seems ready to stab you with it! Here's a universe where an Army general is ridiculed for daring to think that he could one day be president. I mean, an Army general? Okay, maybe a convicted retarded rapist on death row. But to tweak an Army general with such a purple nurple of scorn?

Because, hey, if an Army general is being too uppity by fancying himself a president, who am I? I mean, I'm just a regular joe. Before I've even begun the article, George Will has put me in my place with his scorn, threatens me with a pikestaff if I step out of line, and stands angrily behind the barricade of his bowtie like a line of Chicago cops behind their shields at the 68 Democratic Convention. I don't even deserve to read the article, let alone think about, or—god forbid—think critically about it.

What we are told from the very beginning of the column is that democracy itself is a fraud. In reality, responsible people are either George Will-like in their rarified bowtie and pikestaff universe, dispensing the ideas and judging who is worthy of discussing them, or else they are the rank and file who know their place, which is to keep their stupid mouths shut and pay attention while the George Wills dictate from their bowtie tower.

But remember, the bowtie is only there to keep the feverish head attached to the motorized boll weevil body. He's nothing more than a peevish little toy, wheeling and skittering about in his box. And the thing that keeps him wound up and his gears spinning is his fear, his fear of democracy. His fear that the people, and not some class of philosopher kings, may possibly have their political way. It's not that he hates the Democrats or loves the Republicans. It's just that he hates people. He thinks they're stupid and dangerous. As I suppose they are. He's uncomfortable with most of the 300 million or so folks who run around living their lives in the United States, and he's most uncomfortable with the thought that those very people he fears have some crazy idea that democracy is about THEM putting THEIR two cents into the discussion of official policy.

It's not that he's not a man of the people. No. I don't criticize him because he wouldn't be caught dead in a bowling alley, because he's an Ivy League snob. That's not my problem with him, although it is most likely one of his own private problems. My problem with George F. Will is that he's a man of fear, anger, frustration, and vast emptiness. And the only reason I can see for someone to read one of his columns and enjoy it at face value is that that someone needs his own distrust of popular political participation validated.

So, as I see it, George Will is about as un-American as they come. His very essence denounces participatory democracy. So again I come to the question: Why? Why George Will? More specifically, "Why George Will in the mainstream media?" Does it have anything to do with over-concentration of media ownership? Or do the readers of Newsweek sincerely think themselves unworthy of governing themselves to the extent that they enjoy being browbeaten into abdicating that privilege and duty on a semiweekly basis?

It is truly a mystery as enigmatic as the legends of lost Atlantis.

Until next time, I'm Jeff Dorchen and this has been the Moment of Truth. Good day.

Site: mejeffdorchen

URL: http://oblivio.com/mejeffdorchen/index.shtml

Lube Warning

Ali Davis

All of us abuse the hand sanitizer. I know that over-the-counter antibacterial products are bad. I know that it actually develops hideous resistant strains of bacteria. I even did the high school biology experiment where you put penicillin in a petri dish of E. Coli, then watch the zone of inhibition get smaller and smaller as the bacteria learn to eat the stuff for breakfast. I know it is bad, and I don't think it should even be legal to sell it. All of my fellow clerks agree with me, but we all abuse the hand sanitizer. We can't help it.

Contamination is everywhere. I see people sneezing onto the tape cases. They cough wetly into their palms right before handing me change. They squeegee out their ears with their pinkies. They forget about the security cameras downstairs and pick their noses with wild abandon and astonishing force. Still, the only thing that really freaks me out is the semen. Well, OK, the lubricant freaks me out too, but I'm pretty sure that's because of the implied presence of semen.

The only thing we can do is use the hand sanitizer. I use it so much that I lose all finger traction and can't open our plastic bags. I've had days when I've used it so much that I can't even make fingerprints on the glass countertop. It freaks me out, but the thought of not using it is worse.

Sometimes people get animalistic about the tapes. For the real addicts (I'm convinced that porn is like alcohol: some people can stop at just one every now and then, some people just binge on weekends, and some people get genuinely, horribly addicted) the reptilian brain kicks in. They hit the magic portion of the tape and they're done. They pop out the tape and slam in another one, and the next day the stack comes back, unrewound and covered in goo.

Repeat offenders get a note on their file that says "LUBE WARNING." Management policy is that for $6.50 an hour, clerks should not have to deal with the bodily fluids of others. The first time we discreetly but firmly remind the customer that the tapes need to come back clean. The second time we hand him the tape, the Windex, and the paper towels and tell him to clean off the tape in full view of whoever else is at the counter.

It astonishes me that someone could actually forget to clean off his sticky and/or slippery tapes, but what amazes me even more is that people actually have the balls to argue with us about it. They always claim they got the tapes that way. They will actually claim that the spooge in question was missed by both the clerk that checked it in and the clerk that checked it back out, and that they figured what the hell, they'd go ahead and play it, even though it was covered in gel.

One guy brought back a DVD with a big white thumbprint of come on it. He actually tried to argue with me: "That's not mine. I never even played that! I never even took it out of the case!"

I pointed out that the DVD had been put back in the case with the reverse side up, which was where the thumbprint was. The clerk couldn't have checked the tape out to him that way because the serial number is on the front. The guy still tried to protest that sure, maybe he'd picked it up and looked at it but—"Sir," I said, "It's your THUMBPRINT. Do you really want to get into this?" He did not.

I hate it when people argue, but I understand why they do. I don't think there should be any shame in masturbating, but I do think there should be shame in expecting someone with whom you are not very, very close to deal with a wad of your spooge. I think they get all defensive because in that moment, they realize it too, but I think there's more to it than that.

One of my favorite concepts in anthropology is that of the polite fiction. It's something nobody believes, but we all pretend to because it makes life so much easier. My favorite example was of a Pygmy couple. Pygmy divorce involves quite literally breaking up the home: the couple tears apart their house (it's easy—the houses are made of leaves) and once it's down, the union is dissolved. One anthropologist was watching a long-married couple have a fight. It escalated until the wife threatened to leave, and the husband yelled something along the lines of "Fine!" and there was nothing the wife could do but start tearing down the house. She began tearing the roof off, clearly miserable. The husband looked wretched too, but at this point neither could back down without losing face and by now the whole village was watching.

Finally, the husband called out the Pygmy equivalent of "You're right, honey! The roof is dirty! It'll look much better once we get those leaves washed!" The two of them started carrying leaves down to the river, soon with the help of the whole village, and then washed and rebuilt the whole roof. When the anthropologist later discreetly asked how often one washes the roof, everyone looked at him like he was a complete doofus.

The polite fiction of the porn section is that, while people do generally use porn for the purpose of masturbation, there is no reason to believe that this particular customer will be doing so. He could be using them for his Master's thesis. Hell, he may not get around to watching them at all. We all like to believe that. When it becomes all too clear to everyone involved that said customer did, in fact, not only lube up, watch the tape, stroke himself to orgasm, and then grab the goddamned thing without even taking the basic courtesy of washing his goddamned hands first, we all get uncomfortable.

On the other hand, he gets angry because he's ashamed of something that was entirely avoidable and his own fault. I'm supposed to keep my temper even though I've just put my hand in a wad of his semen.

The destruction of the polite fiction is what creeps me out about one of my weekend regulars. He comes in when I open at nine, then chooses and rents two movies. He leaves for exactly two movies' worth of time, then returns them before four to get the matinee special. I hate it because there's no way to pretend he's been doing anything else. I just hope to God there's been a hand washing between him and me. I think there is, because his tapes are always clean, but it still gives me the shivvers and sends me straight to the hand sanitizer. It's just too much to know.

Mr. Glasses is the very creepiest, though. He's always very friendly, even courtly. He's too friendly, actually—he's always doing stuff like announcing "It's THAT kind of personal service that sets your store apart from the Blockbusters!" Yeah, whatever. The over-friendliness itself is creepy, as is the way he sort of doesn't blink enough and doesn't know that most business transactions don't really involve sustained eye contact. (No, he's not hitting on me. He's gay.) But of course what puts him over the top is that he's our biggest repeat lube offender. I hate seeing him coming. It's like Russian Roulette.

Rainy days are the worst. He just plunks a wet bag on the counter and we have to reach in and get the tapes. You know that initiation ritual in Flash Gordon where the guy has to stick his hand way, way down a hole and usually it's fine but sometimes there's a venemous beastie at the end that stings him? It's like that. Actually, it isn't quite. The tapes are always a bit wet on rainy days—it's just that my brain can't stop churning about what they might be wet with.

We all abuse the hand sanitizer. And I am deeply grateful that it exists.

Site: True Porn Clerk Stories

URL: http://www.improvisation.ws/mb/showthread.php?s=&threadid=4475

Jon's Wife

Heather B. Armstrong

So this telemarketer from Sears just called and asked for Jon. And since I knew immediately that it was a telemarketer I told her no, he wasn't here, but if she'd like to leave her name and home telephone number, I'm sure he'd love to call her back at an inconvenient time. And I don't think she even heard me because she just sort of ignored me and said, "Well then, is Jon's wife available?"

And normally I would have said no, but I couldn't help but wonder how she knew that he was married, and if she knew that much information, what else did she know?

So I said, "Yes, I am Jon's wife," and before I could ask her how she knew that he was married, or if she also knew that he has a chronically unmanageable thicket of curls covering his entire head, or that he can't sleep in past 7:30 AM on any given morning, and that when he wakes up he has the cutest uncontrollable urge to tap me and nuzzle my neck even though I'm usually grumpy and covered in a thick film of my own morning breath, or that he bought me Mother's Day presents on behalf of the dog, or that he can stand to be around my family even though they're abrasively Southern and very into plastic plants, or that he can wield a weed whacker LIKE NOBODY"S BUSINESS, or that he has such a remarkable relationship with the dog that the dog will only go pee if he is standing nearby, or that he hits his head on the heating ducts every single time he goes into the basement and vows that he is going to cover those fuckers with foam but never gets around to it, or that he has the most beautiful hands, perfectly aged and rough from working every day of his life and that there is nothing more satisfying in this life than to look down and see those hands gripping my waist, or that he can stand a certain way when he comes home from work, slightly angular, his arms heavy from fatigue, and that it makes my heart beat so fast that I can burn an entire package of Twizzler's Cherry Nibs worth of calories just by looking at him...

Before I could ask her any of this, she made the monumental mistake of asking, "Well, does he allow you to answer his phone calls?"

And I know she didn't mean any offense, or at least for a split second I gave her the benefit of the doubt and assumed she didn't mean any offense, but after that single split second I gave into the hackles on the back of my neck and answered rather lovingly into the speaker phone, "I'm not sure about that lady, but I am sure that your husband ALLOWS you to be a cunt."

And if she didn't know before, she knows now that Jon allows me to use such language.

Site: Dooce

URL: http://dooce.com

Spare Us The Cutter

Wil Wheaton

The call came while I was out, so I didn't get the message until days later.

"Hi," the young-sounding secretary said on my machine, "I have Rick Berman calling for Wil. Please return when you get the message."

I knew.

I knew before she was even done with the message, but I tried to fool myself for a few minutes anyway. I looked at the clock: 8 PM. They'd most likely be out, so I'd have to call tomorrow. I told Anne that I had a message to call Rick's office, and she knew right away also.

We'd thought about it for months, ever since I'd heard the rumors online. Of course, I tend to not put a whole lot of stock in what I read online...if I did I'd be overwhelmed with the sheer amount of hot teen bitches who want to get naked for me right now, and I'd be rolling in Nigerian money.

But it made sense, and I couldn't fight what I knew in my heart to be true.

I returned the call late the next day from my car on my way home from work. I was driving along a narrow tree-lined street in Pasadena that I sometimes take when the traffic is heavy on the freeway. Children played on bikes and jumped rope in the growing shadows of the July afternoon. The street was stained a beautiful orange by the setting sun.

"This is Wil Wheaton returning," I told her.

She tells me to hold on, and then he's on the phone.

"Hi kiddo. How are you?"

"I'm doing fine. You know I turn 30 on Monday?"

There is a pause.

"I can't believe we're all getting so old," he says.

"I know. I emailed Tommy [his son] awhile ago, and he's in college now. If that made me feel old, I can't imagine what my turning 30 is doing to the rest of you guys."

We chuckle. This is probably just small-talk, so it's not as severe when he tells me, but it feels good regardless. Familiar, familial.

"Listen, Wil. I have bad news."

Although I've suspected it for months, and I have really known it since I heard the message the night before, my stomach tightens, my arms grow cold.

"We've had to cut your scene from the movie."

He pauses for breath, and that moment is frozen, while I assess my feelings.

I almost laugh out loud at what I discover: I feel puzzled.

I feel puzzled, because the emotions I expected: the sadness, the anger, the indignation...aren't there.

I realize that he's waiting for me.

"Why'd you have to cut it?"

This doesn't make sense. I should be furious. I should be depressed. I should be hurt.

But I don't feel badly, at all.

"Well, it doesn't have anything to do with you," he begins.

I laugh silently. It never does. When I don't get a part, or a callback, or get cut from a movie, it never has anything to do with me. Like a sophmore romance. "It's not you. It's me. I've met Jimmy Kimmel's cousin, and things just happened."

There is an unexpected sincerity to what he tells me: the movie is long. The first cut was almost 3 hours. The scene didn't contribute to the main story in any way, so it was the first one to go.

He tells me that they've cut 48 minutes from the movie.

I tell him that they've cut an entire episode out. We laugh.

There is another silence. He's waiting for me to respond.

I drive past some kids playing in an inflatable pool in their front yard. On the other side of the street, neighbors talk across a chain link fence. An older man sits on his porch reading a paper.

"Well Rick," I begin, "I completely understand. I've thought about this on and off for months, and I knew that if the movie was long, this scene, and maybe even this entire sequence, would have to go. It's just not germaine to the spine of the story."

He tells me that they had to consider cutting the entire beginning of the movie. He tells me that he has to call one of the other actors because they've suffered rather large cuts as well.

I stop at a 4-way stop sign and let a woman and her little daughter cross the street on their way into a park filled with families, playing baseball and soccer in the waning light.

I look them. The mother's hand carefully holding her daughter's. I realize why I'm not upset, and I tell him.

"Well, Rick, it's like this: I love Star Trek, and, ultimately, I want what's best for Star Trek and the Trekkies. If the movie is too long, you've got to cut it, and this scene is the first place I'd start if I were you.

"The great thing is, I got to spend two wonderful days being on Star Trek again, working with the people I love, wearing the uniform that I missed, and I got to re-connect with you, the cast, and the fans. Nobody can take that away from me."

"And, it really means a lot to me that you called me yourself. I can't tell you how great that makes me feel,"

It's true. He didn't need to call me himself. Most producers wouldn't.

"I'm so glad that you took the time to call me, and that I didn't have to learn about this at the screening, or by reading it on the internet."

He tells me again how sorry he is. He asks about my family, and if I'm working on anything. I tell him they're great, that Ryan's turning 13, and that I've been enjoying steady work as a writer since January.

We're back to small talk again, bookending the news.

I ask him how the movie looks.

He tells me that they're very happy with it. He thinks it's going to be very successful.

I'm feel happy and proud.

I've heard stories from people that everyone had lots of trouble with the director. I ask him if that's true.

He tells me that it was tough, because the director had his own vision. There were struggles, but ultimately they collaborated to make a great film.

I come to a stoplight, a bit out of place in this quiet residential neighborhood. A young married couple walks their golden retriever across the crosswalk.

We say our goodbyes, and he admonishes me to call him if I'm ever on the lot. He tells me that he'll never forgive me if I don't stop into his office when I'm there.

I tell him that I will, and that I'll see him at the screening.

He wishes me well, and we hang up the phone.

The light turns green and I sit there for a moment, reflecting on the conversation.

I think back to something I wrote in April while in a pit of despair: "I wonder if The Lesson is that, in order to succeed, I need to rely upon myself, trust myself, love myself, and not put my happiness and sadness into the hands of others."

I meant everything that I said to him. It really doesn't matter to me if I'm actually in the movie or not, and not in a bitter way at all.

I could focus on the disappointment, I suppose. I could feel sad.

Getting cut out of the movie certainly fits a pattern that's emerged in the past two years or so.

But I choose not to. I choose instead to focus on the positives, the things I can control. I did have two wonderful days with people I love, and it was like I'd never left. I did get to reconnect with the fans and the franchise. Rick Berman, a person with whom I've not always had the best relationship, called me himself to tell me the news, and I felt like it weighed heavily on him to deliver it.

Nobody can take that away from me, and I'm not going to feel badly, at all.

Because I have a secret.

I have realized what's important in my life since April, and they are at the end of my drive.

The dog-walking couple smile and wave to me.

The light changes.

Somewhere in Brooklyn, Wesley Crusher falls silent forever.

Site: Wil Wheaton Dot Net

URL: http://wilwheaton.net

Interview with Wil Wheaton of Wil Wheaton Dot Net

When you say the name Wil Wheaton most people instantly think of kid-genius Wesley Crusher on *Star Trek: The Next Generation*. Or perhaps as the boy racing across railroad tracks in the movie *Stand By Me*. However thanks to blogging, Wheaton seems to have found a permanent niche as an author. His fandom has only grown since he left the *Star Trek* series and went online with his everyday adventures in life after child stardom. Wheaton recently signed a three-book deal with O'Reilly & Associates that includes two books based on his blog: Dancing Barefoot, and Just A Geek. Both books are filled with autobiographical narrative non-fiction about his experiences as a geek, husband, stepfather, and former Star Trek actor.

Why did you feel compelled to write about your experiences online?

Because I spent the first part of my life in the public eye, many people had a skewed impression of who I was. I saw an opportunity to speak for myself with my blog, and dispel many of the misconceptions people had about me. After I'd been blogging for about a year, I realized that I'd been heavily influenced by the same misconceptions, and writing honestly about them helped me exorcise many demons, and find my Path in life.

What has the reaction been from people regarding your blog?

Overall, it's been very positive. Many people have told me that they've been inspired by my struggles and successes in acting and writing, or by my love for my wife and stepchildren.

Have your TV fans been as accepting toward your newfound Web stardom?

I am very uncomfortable with the idea of "my fans." It implies some sort of ownership, and creates this weird responsibility to do stuff for "my fans." The same goes for "stardom." Whether Web or TV or film-based, "stardom" is fleeting. If I start thinking about "my fans" and "stardom," I stop writing for me and my Ideal Reader, and start worrying about how I can keep "my fans" happy, so my "stardom" doesn't fade. I already experience the hollow pursuit of fame when I was an idiot teenager, and I'm not going to do that again. The way I look at it now, I'm very fortunate that people like to read what I like to write, and for some reason I'm able to touch something in those readers.

What have you learned from your transition from TV into an author?

Well, I haven't written nearly enough to consider myself an author. Maybe in a few years, if I'm able to get some good fiction out there, and consistently turn out quality material, I'll call myself an author. Right now, I'm just an aspiring writer. Because of my limited experience with writing, and the unique way I do it (blogging, mostly) I don't have a good sense of what real authors go through. I can tell you that so far it's more fulfilling from a creative standpoint. In television and movies, there are several steps between the performance on the set, and the final result on the screen. There are countless opportunities for the performance to become better or worse: cutting, music, lighting, other actors' reactions, the scenes preceding and following mine . . . if the thing I did on the set is similar to what an audience sees, it's very rare. Because of that, there are numerous "outs" for me as an actor if the performance sucks, or the movie tanks. However, as a writer, there's only one editor between the audience and myself, and I have the final word on what goes into print. Because of that, I can own the successes more, but I also have total responsibility for the failures, too. It's much more risky, but at the end of the day it's much more "real" than television or movies.

Why do you think blogging has become so popular in the last few years?

Well, I think you'd have to look real hard to find people who don't like to talk about themselves, for starters. Also, we live in a world that is just so . . . noisy . . . and individual, unpopular, and dissenting voices have been all but silenced by a consolidated media that seems to broadly paint the world into binary black and white contrasts. Blogs provide an opportunity for anyone with a voice to use it. It's what the Internet was intended to be: a tool to communicate and share information quickly and easily.

Do you read other people's online journals? If so, who? If not, why?

I am severely limited by time, but I read several political blogs almost daily, including alternet.org, talkingpointsmemo.com, cursor.org, and thismodernworld.com. I also read Andy Inhatko's blog, Paul Ford, and Neil Gaiman.

How has blogging changed your life?

I see the world in literary terms now. When something cool happens that I want to share, I want to have good language to do it. I often catch myself narrating in my head.

What do you hope people learn about you from your writing?

I'm just this guy, you know?

1999

Matthew Baldwin

I was getting my hair cut by a young lady at the local barber shop.

Her: What day is it today?

Me: Um, Thursday.

Her: Wow, it's almost the end of the week—it's almost the end of the month, even! And next month I turn 21! I can't believe it!

Me: Sneaks up on you, huh?

Her: It's crazy! I mean, how can I be 21?! How can it already be 2003?!

Me: Uh-huh.

Her: I mean, do you remember when that song came out, that "1999" song by that guy?

Me: Prince?

Her: Yeah. Do you remember when that song first came out, how they played it, like, all the time? And then New Year's came and it was the year 2000 and they totally stopped playing it? I mean, that seems like yesterday.

Me: When 1999 *first* came out?

Her: Yeah. Do you remember that? A few years ago?

The haircut cost 20 bucks, but the feeling old was free.

Site: Defective Yeti

URL: http://defectiveyeti.com

Last Night At The Grocery Store

Mrs. Kennedy

Last night at the grocery store, as Jackson was trying to run my driver's license through the credit card machine and I was struggling to keep him from (a) falling off the check writing thingy and (b) canceling my whole transaction, the guy who bags the groceries smiled at both of us and said, Paper or plastic? The bag guy: a little scruffy, and tall, and in no hurry. Also, about nineteen years old. Jackson is wiggling like a mother now and I have three bags full, and when our guy says most capably, Do you need help getting out to your car? I think, You need to come with us. I say, That would be great. He is so ready to help, I could probably suggest lots of things and maybe he'd say okay. He picks up our bags and walks out with us. Jackson is brandishing my driver's license. He throws it into the street. Tallboy bends to pick it up, shyly gives it back to me. Carefully loads the bags into my trunk and closes it. I would eat him alive, there'd be nothing left but teeth and hair. He's not ready to go back in to work, but I'm not going anywhere but home. He and Jackson wave bye to each other. Jackson sits in his car seat and sings his favorite song. Hey baby, hey baby, hey. I have been flirting with a stranger. And it makes me happy for a little while.

But then I get home and think, Am I having a midlife crisis?

And Jack comes home and says, Do you want to watch American Beauty?

Statistically, you're probably not going to spend an hour and a half fucking someone you've been with for eight years. But it can happen, and while it does you won't be thinking about scruffy grocery clerks.

Who needs sleep? Hey baby, hey.

Site: Fussy

URL: http://whatsthefuss.com

Darth Vader Made Me Cry

Matthew Baldwin

When I was seven years old I received the best Christmas present ever: a copy of The Star Wars Storybook. On the inside front cover my parents had written "To Matthew—Merry Christmas in 1978. From Mother and Daddy with lots of love."

I was fairly certain that this was a gift beyond improvement. But a few months later I saw in the paper that Darth Vader—*the* Darth Vader!—would be coming to a nearby department store. I begged my mom to take me. She agreed, and we visited the mall on a Saturday afternoon so I could get Vader's John Hancock.

Upon our arrival we found ourselves at the end of a long line of parents and youngsters eagerly waiting their opportunity to meet Darth Vader. Kids would be allowed to approach Vader singly or in small groups; they would approach and exchange a few words, or ask for autographs, or simply stand there awe-struck. It was like visiting Santa Claus, except the guest of honor was more renowned for breaking necks than for dispensing candy canes. And, to the best of my knowledge, no one sits on Darth Vader's lap.

As I got closer to the front of the line, I could feel my excitement reach fever pitch. Finally it was my turn. The attendant waved me through, and I rushed forward to meet my anti-hero. But once I actually entered Darth Vader's Personal Space, I was abruptly cowed. He was huge! And he had exactly the sort of dominating presence you'd expect of an Imperial Dark Lord. I was struck dumb, and stood there like a field mouse that had just spotted an owl.

At some point I managed to squeak out my request—or maybe I just held the book and black marker out, I honestly don't recall. In any case, Darth Vader took the Storybook, quickly wrote something inside, and handed it back. I stammered out a thank you as we were ushered off to the side.

As we walked away I was filled with combination of terror, relief, and exhilaration. After snapping out of my daze I urged my mother to stop walking so I could see the autograph, and opened the storybook to find the words "Darth Vader" scrawled on the inside cover. I immediately began to proactively gloat, thinking about how jealous my friends would be when I showed them Darth Vader's autograph. But then, just before I closed the cover, I noticed something else. While signing my book, he had also taken the opportunity to scratch out the word "love" in the inscription "From Mother and Daddy with lots of love."

Stunned that the Lord of Sith could be so mean I immediately burst into tears, and continued to bawl as my mother led me to the escalator. The kids still in line watched me with curiosity, and then glanced at Darth Vader with fear in their eyes.

Site: Defective Yeti

URL: http://defectiveyeti.com

Alabama Hamilton

Heather B. Armstrong

My sister's name is September, and today is her 32nd birthday. Yes, that's right. My parents named my sister September even though she was born in January, and she has consequently suffered years of obvious questions. Of course, these are the same people who named their only son Ranger.

I know you're wondering, how the hell did I end up with the boring name, because everyone who knows about my siblings mindlessly blurts out, "How did you get stuck with the boring name?" as if I had anything to do with it or haven't ever heard that question before.

I really hate that question. It's like asking someone, "How did you get so ugly?"

Considering the amount of teasing my brother and sister endured during childhood, I've never really felt cheated that I got stuck with the boring name. September lucked out, really, because in early 1970, a week before she was born, my father decided that they should name her Mangis Colorado whether she ended up being a boy or a girl.

Mangis.

There's no city in Colorado called Mangis. There is, however, a horse named Mangis, and this horse was apparently my father's favorite character in a movie about someone in the Old West who shot a lot of people.

Ranger was named after a box of cigars my father saw at a truck stop in the middle of Arkansas. It took my mother two weeks to talk my Dad down from Ranger Cigars to just Ranger. He finally agreed that Ranger Cigars in its entirety would be a bit suspicious since Mormons aren't supposed to smoke. It would be like a Catholic family naming their child Nurse Orthotricyclen, or something.

When I finally came along in 1975 I think either Dad was just exhausted, what with having to name two whole children before me, or Mom subconsciously knew that I would be a special case, and that a peculiar name would really only make things worse.

I mean, seriously. Who wouldn't make fun a sixth grade bra-stuffing, know-it-all named Alabama Hamilton?

I know I would.

Site: Dooce

URL: http://dooce.com

Interview with Heather Armstrong of Dooce

Freelance Web designer Heather Armstrong had no idea a blog could get her into so much trouble. One day she's writing about her frustrations at work, and the next day she's out of a job for generating online sympathy on her blog Dooce.com. Now a freelancer and mom-to-be, Heather reflects on blogging and freedom of speech.

Why did you feel compelled to write about your experiences online?

I think I feel compelled to write online much for the same reasons a musician likes to play in a band and perform in front of an audience or to cut an album and release it to audiences. There is something very satisfying about sharing myself in a creative way with a relatively large group of strangers who might potentially find something of their own experience in what I'm trying to express. Having an audience motivates me to write more than I would if I didn't have one. I think "bloggers" or anyone who keeps a personal website have a bad reputation as being narcissistic or self-important because we think our opinions and feelings have some sort of significance just by virtue of putting them online for others to read.

And although I don't think we're exempt from self-importance—we have to have a little bit of an ego in order to have the courage to put ourselves out there for public consumption, usually without getting paid to do so—I think there is a fundamental human desire to share and express and communicate with others, and I think most people who run personal websites operate on that fundamental urge. And what a wonderful tool the Internet is to facilitate this desire.

I also look at my website as a creative project in which I get to wear many different hats. I get to write it, edit it, design it, code it, and tweak it all to my own specifications. It's the most creatively fulfilling thing I've ever done.

What has the reaction been from people regarding your blog reporting?

I think most people who read my website understand what I'm trying to do, that I'm just trying to share stories about life in a creative way. Occasionally I get email from people who take my website too literally or too seriously, people who either have no sense of humor or are looking to be upset about something. And they have every right to be upset or to take offense at something I've written, but I think they are completely missing the point.

When it comes down to it, it's just a personal website, and I'm not out to change the world. It's just my little art project that I hope others can enjoy.

During the first year of the website when I was trying to figure out my voice and style of writing I was very naive in thinking that everyone would understand that I'm just writing stories, stories with exaggerated characters, stories that should be read more as anecdotes than as a completely literal record of my life. During that first year I wrote several entries about work-related themes with characters based on people I had worked with over five or six years at various Internet/start-up companies.

I was genuinely frustrated with my job and with working in a corporate environment, but the stories I wrote about it on my website weren't meant to slander anyone personally or to bad mouth the company I was working for at the time. And I never mentioned anyone by name (particularly because most of the characters were sketched from more than one person I had worked with) and I never mentioned any company or product by name. I didn't share any trade secrets or violate any non-disclosure agreement.

When an anonymous person emailed every vice-president of the company I worked for and informed them that I was maintaining this personal website, some of the vice-presidents found it funny, but others were furious. The president of the company ordered that I be fired immediately, probably because the company was about to seek an additional round of venture capital, and he didn't want anything "negative" going on in the company. I completely understand why I lost my job, but I wasn't even given a warning or a chance to take down any entries that they thought were dangerous to the image of the company. And even though it happened almost two years ago, I'm still astounded that my little art project caused such a massive ripple.

What did you learn from the experience?

I get a lot of e-mail from people seeking advice on whether or not they should be worried about something they've written on their website about work or family. I cannot emphasize enough that writing about work on a personal website is not a good idea, unless it has been officially sanctioned by a boss or a supervisor, or if there is some written policy that details specifically what can and cannot be said about the workplace on a blog. If someone is unwilling to tell their boss about what he/she is saying about work on their personal website, then he/she should stop writing about work immediately if they care at all about the security of their job. I hope others learn from what happened to me, that you could lose your job for something as benign as writing humorous stories with characters loosely based and sketched on people you work with. As far as family and friends go, I never publish anything on my website about people in my personal life that I wouldn't say to their faces.

What do you hope people learn about you from your writing?

I hope people can find something of their own experience in what I write, and I hope that sometimes I can articulate, at least in the fuzzy, intangible Internet world, what a lot of people want to say but are afraid to say. I hope people know that even though I exaggerate almost everything and squeeze every bit of drama I can out of a situation, that I'm fundamentally trying to be honest, to communicate an honest feeling. I want people to know that behind the bitchy, hard-edged Dooce persona is a deeply emotional and sensitive woman who isn't afraid to talk about depression or religion or disease or the daily trauma of certain bodily functions. I want people to know that I write because I want to share and connect and laugh and cry.

Why do you think blogging has become so popular in the last few years?

Personal publishing is so easy and so available and so powerful, at least in terms of giving one person's voice an instant stage and audience. Blogging is so empowering that even the most shy and introverted person can march out his/her opinions and convictions and experiences without feeling the actual physical uneasiness that comes with doing it face to face. This can be both a good and bad thing, as people feel freer to be mean and vindictive and nasty behind the wall of the Internet than they would if they were holding a face-to-face conversation with someone. But ultimately, I think personal publishing is an amazing equalizer. Anyone with access to an Internet connection and the will to do it can publish themselves online.

Do you read other people's online journals? If so, who? If not, why?

I am addicted to about 50 different blogs, and I check them multiple times a day for updates. There are the usual names, such as Kottke.org, which one should read just to maintain blog currency, to know at any given moment what is going on in this arena. I read Textism (Dean Allen), Openbrackets (Gail Armstrong), Fireland (Josh Allen), The Morning News, Heather Champ (hchamp.com), Oblivio (Michael Barrish), Ftrain (Paul Ford), What Do I Know (Todd Dominey), Leslie Harpold, Melanie Goux (Brushstroke.tv), Dollarshort

(Mena Trott), Anil Dash, Dive Into Mark (Mark Pilgrim), Maciej Ceglowski (Idlewords), Todd Levin (Tremble), IzzlePfaff, Mighty Girl (Margaret Barry), Coudal Partners, Zeldman, my husband (Blurbomat), Shauny.org, and many, many others. My favorite personal website is QueSeraSera (Sarah Brown), who never fails to make me laugh or punch me in the gut.

What are you working on when you're not busy blogging?

My husband and I just finished remodeling our kitchen and putting the final touches on a nursery, all in preparation for our first child. Although being pregnant can at times feel like a full-time job, I've been doing freelance design for several clients I took with me when I moved from LA to Utah. Right now, however, I'm working on trying to relax and to stop folding and refolding the baby's sock drawer. I think once my hands stop moving I'll have to really think about having this baby, and actually having to think about it will totally freak me out. I need more time. Nine months is not nearly enough time to fully comprehend the whole "making of life" thing.

‘DID HE DO IT?”

Greg Apt

“DID HE DO IT?”

This is the question my friends most commonly ask me when asking me about cases. The question is actually hard to answer sometimes.

As a PD, I don’t get to choose my cases, they are assigned to me randomly (through some matrix system depending on what court I am working in) or, in the more serious cases, assigned to me by a supervisor who looks at my caseload and determines it’s time for me to work a little harder. Turning a case down is not an option (at least not more than once. Maybe you can pull a “personal reason” excuse once, but don’t try more than that).

But the question of “did he do it” is a complex one. For the most part, my clients did something wrong to get themselves into custody. The only question is what did they do, and does the provable actions conform to the charges against them? Thus, while my client may have possessed drugs, and should be found guilty of that (a truly absurd crime, but that’s another post), the client should be found not guilty of possessing them for purposes of sale. This can have a huge distinction in Cal. In some cases it can be the difference between a small fine and life in prison (in the case of pot, the difference between a \$100 fine and life in prison can be a cop disliking you and “opining” that you possessed that eighth for purposes of sale). So, did he do it?

Even in more severe cases such a conundrum exists. In a murder case, maybe my client shot the person, but did so in self-defense. So, yes, he did kill the person, but we will argue that it was not murder, and the DA will argue that it was.

Ultimately, I was not there for any of these crimes (if I was, it would be a conflict of interest for me to represent the person since I would also be a witness). I can only rely on what I read in the reports and hear from the witnesses. Sometimes, the overwhelming evidence convinces even me conclusively that my client “did it,” despite his consistent denials. Other times, I can only throw up my hands and say “I dunno, we’ll have to let the jury decide.”

I used to feel in just about every instance that there was at least some truth to what an officer testified about when they say my client committed a crime, or they found evidence on him. Rampart began to change my mind (if you don't know what Rampart is by now, go to the LA Weekly web site, or do a google search, but essentially it was the largest scandal in LA history for corrupt cops planting evidence and falsely testifying against defendants in central LA). I actually had some cases with these cops, and I had no reason to believe that they would just go and plant evidence on completely innocent people. I figured they shaded the truth at times, exaggerated to get someone convicted, but make stuff up wholesale???? I guess even cynical I didn't want to believe that. Well, it happened.

So, if my client says that he didn't have those drugs the police say they found on him, who am I to tell him he's a liar. And who am I to tell someone, when they ask, that he "did it"?

Site: Public Defender Dude

URL: http://publicdefenderdude.blogspot.com/

Romance

Mrs. Kennedy

I've always had a terrible time believing in romance. When I was 9 or 10 years old I remember giving my parents a little survey to try and figure out what they had in common—I truly didn't understand what kept them together. I came to the conclusion that they stayed together because they both liked to play cards.

Site: Fussy

URL: http://whatsthefuss.com

Celebrity

Choire Sicha

Like two avenging Rapunzels high in the vertiginous brick towers of their massive London Terrace apartment complex, Susan Sontag and Annie Liebowitz gaze down upon Manhattan. Often (of course, before their alleged estrangement), I would picture them knitting an endless kaffiyeh-and-dollar-sign-patterned scarf in their vine-crusted rooftop garden. In my mind, Susan would pause in her knitting to lean against a gargoyle, fixing her Mothra radar gaze to Tenth Avenue in fond protection of conceptually-pure ideologues. Across the patio, Annie, our avatar of photographic commerce, rests her multiple blue arms whilst x-ray scanning the desolate cross-streets for the best facial structures.

Perhaps the third of these Furies is Deborah Harry, fellow London Terrace resident. She of course is the patron saint of the low-slung-pants-wearing art school video artists, those last carriers of a spark of artistic fire bound to soon be crushed in the faultline between the rupturing techtonic plates of money and power. I picture Debbie Harry, the last great American poet now retired, wearing only motorcycle boots and a white slip, thrashing about on her bed in a dank apartment (on a much lower floor than Annie and Susan) in torment at the punishment that inevitably will come to all those who aspire to blinding-white fame. Despite her daily fevers, she believes there is life in this life in the arts, and so she rises nightly in a shimmering silver dress and unbelievable heels, always ready to rock. There is hope in this tundra, Debbie Harry, Debbie Harry!

In a secret location, perhaps deposed to an attic Kew Gardens, Fran Lebowitz rots in an overstuffed yellow Edwardian chair. A bottle of Night Train slips to the floor from the stuffing under the chair. Her mansuit is musty and threadbare. Like a poet she ashes in her pantlegs. Like a poet, she nibbles her pencils, half her daylight caloric intake. The last pundit of the glamorous Manhattan life, she now takes the subway. Like a poet, she drinks other people's wine, and also like a poet, she does not actually write.

Laurie Anderson is naked, crouched atop Lou Reed, grinding away like a Nomi Malone. She is eating a banana, her head thrown back, her spiky hair casting a Statue of Liberty shadow on the wall. Lou's naked hairy back is catching on the Mongolian wool bed spread. He is distracted by a lost phrase. He wants to get up and write it down. He thinks there might be a good song in this phrase. The phrase that he can't remember is "Indelible edible you, the first lover of virtue." There's no song there.

Isaac Mizrahi is scooping Harry's shit off Fifth Avenue, using only a green plastic bag. Adam Yauch is eating day-old half-off vegan corn muffins from the Rastafarian Bakery on Lorimer Street. Jon Stewart is in Fort Lee, New Jersey, in a rent-by-the-hour Pink Pussycat motel with a 19-year-old Cuban-Korean transgender prostitute, and he is having the time of his life. Sandy Weill is shuffling on his marble-floored bathroom to a hot Missy Elliott remix. David Byrne is staring down a Norwegian subway accordian player, stealing music with his mind. Megan Mullally is having a lemon-ginger tea in her sunny-yellow kitchen nook, talking to a girlfriend about their first abortions and how much she didn't like Madonna.

And Madonna herself is flopped like a fish on the wooden floor, recovering from a long vinyasa series. Blue veins pulse on her hot forearms. She is thinking: Salad. First the salad. With tuna. Wasabi-vinagrette. Do I have to take a crap again? Wait. Empty the mind. I am a white movie screen. Salad. Empty the mind. Red. What's red. Hollywood lips. Orange. ROY G BIV. Oranges are orange. The Y is for yellow. Yellow: frail women in bonnets in dying apple orchards. Green. Not money. Green is apple Jolly Ranchers. Moving down through the spectrum, the movie screen in Madonna's mind bleaches to a cool static white. Her shoulderblades nestled against each other, she is completely still.

Site: Choire Sicha Dot Com

URL: http://choiresicha.com

Interview with Choire Sicha of Choire Sicha Dot Com

Choire Sicha, editor of Gawker, a Web site obsessed with Manhattan's media and culture, and a contributing writer at *The Morning News* and *The New York Observer*. He's written about everything from the pain of broken hearts to the worse pain of jury duty. In fact, some of his fans of harken him as the next David Sedaris.

Why did you feel compelled to write about your experiences online?

I started this as a way to keep up with my best friend Philo in San Francisco. I don't write letters, and at the time I didn't fly, and I hate talking on the phone, but I wanted to stay close with him. I knew if we wrote each other letters in public we'd feel the pressure. Yeah, we're both exhibitionists. Plus I love deadlines—if I know I have to write something, I will. Shame is the best motivator. We did this for, sheesh, two years? A little more? And it was great for me, writing every day—over the course of two years, I went from being a really crappy writer to having an understanding of the basics of sentence structure.

It was also really embarrassing, and I hated people reading it. I was working things out in public, and it was really overly revealing and I'm a terribly shy person in my exhibitionistic way and it was very, very uncomfortable at times. I hated it a lot, and some of it was really, really fun. He's a good instigator, too. He kept me on track.

Do you read other people's online journals? If so, who? If not, why?

Yeah, but only the good ones. Heh. I read hundreds of weblogs and lots of journals. There's lots of impressive writers online, some of whom are getting print recognition now (if that counts as validation, because why not write online as an end in itself?), some of who are just having a grand old time. Dana at bobofett.com was an early inspiration. She's a really free, seat of the pants comedy writer. Leslie Harpold and Lance Arthur are now old-school online writers who were inspirational. And my girl Blaise at bazima.com. I like the freaky people: Richard at panchesco.com, Jennie at mrtrinity.eastwest.nu, and also folks like Paul Ford and Josh Allen and Matthew Baldwin, et al, at The Morning News, who also keep personal sites. Matthew Baldwin in particular is insanely funny. Skot at izzlepfaff.com. Michael at oblivio.com. The list could go on and on.

Why do you think blogging has become so popular in the last few years?

I think blogging has become popular because public creation brings a sense of satisfaction unlike anything else, and this format is the easiest way to perform in public since singing in the subway. I also think most blogs have a short lifespan because most people don't have time or inclination to develop the skills necessary to write. Trying to say something is frustrating, particularly when you don't know how—and where the hell would we learn, public school? I'd still like to go back to Evanston Township High School and kick my journalism teacher's ass. Me, I don't believe that naturally good writers are born, I believe in discipline. I still have to fight my brain and bad habits to write a sentence—not even a good sentence, just a sentence—and I write thousands of words every week.

What has the reaction been from people regarding your online writing?

Horror, mostly.

Seriously, the non-edited immediate-publication revolution allows the writer a whole new sort of feedback—non-edited immediate feedback, usually. It's harsh. And if you can take it—or worse, take the silence surrounding a misguided piece of writing—you'll improve.

What do you hope people learn about you from your writing?

I really like extremely personal non-fiction, but as I branch out into reported work, I find I want people to know less and less about me. The very nature of weblogging is writing about one's self, not others; this is perhaps its most interesting feature and greatest shortcoming. We don't all regard ourselves fairly, realistically, or with any great insight. (I love that about us—we don't know ourselves very well.)

Here's something I think about though: we all walk around our towns—Manhattan, for me—feeling like a mess, a loser, a slob, whatever, and all around us everyone looks all shiny and successful and loved. But then check into a weblog, where you can see the pretty exterior veneer all peeled down. It's a bit of everyone's insides outside.

Known In The Gates

Allison Lowe

My history as a vigilante is long and storied.

When I was in junior high school, I had this friend who was a boy. We were in a few classes together and had a big time laughing it up and snickering behind our notebooks at our social studies teacher, who once spelled, on the chalkboard, the word "attracts" as "attracks." He was a jewel of the educational system, a coach who later was jailed for his inappropriate relationships with members of the baseball team.

Anyway, this friend of mine, let's call him "Matt," because that is his name, changed his tune on me when we hit the big leagues of high school. With the benefit of hindsight, I can see we had these sweet crushes on each other, but then got to high school and didn't have any classes together and he played football and, you know, things are different when you get mixed in with all these older kids in a new place, back on the bottom rung and making allegiances wherever you can to get ahead in the food chain. So, we drifted. Somehow, I took extreme offense at this. I can't even remember all the details now, but the two of us had this other, mutual friend, a girl, who acted as a go between, of sorts, since we never saw each other anymore and she saw both of us. Now I can see what an Iago she was, always telling me things he said, little barbs pieced out by her, designed to offend me, if only slightly, that built up over time to make me sick with rejection. Elizabeth, snake that she was, who just thought Matt was the end-all of cool, chose him over me—a good choice when looking solely at rankings—and made her cuts where she could to assure that our separation was permanent. Such bad blood was pooling on my side of the thing, for the entire first semester of high school, I was having a hard time getting past it.

That's when I met some snakes of my own, and, like a light coming on (or going off), everything changed.

Back in jr. high I had been ill-fated to be a member of the Losingest Girl's Basketball Team in history. In the trenches with me were Tito and LBJ, two best friends from grade school who were more competitive than any boys I had ever seen and smarter, by leagues, than just about anyone. We were passing friends, but our devotion was not cemented until those dark days of my freshman year when somehow we ended up rejoined in Mrs. Annie B. Holt's Algebra I class.

Ten volumes could be written about the mathematical stylings I received therein, but let's move on to the topic at hand. Tito and LBJ and I, thrown in together like this, could not help but become a unit. They listened and sympathized in regard to what I perceived to be the betrayal of a friend, and slowly, a plan for redemption began to emerge.

The only way for me to overcome my pain, apparently, was to roll Matt's yard. I believe in other parts of our nation, people call it "toilet-papering a yard." That's calling it what it is, I guess. Nothing else was going to do it. Revenge, writ large in streaming white streaks, was the only answer. To my ninth-grade mind, this made perfect sense. I wasn't usually one for vandalism, but when Tito drew out a diagram and calculated the TP to tree ratio, I saw how the scheme could work.

Our strategies were varied and complicated. Much exchange went on in areas physical ("The coverage of his yard is not good. If a car drives by, what is the plan? How do you actually get the paper in the trees?") to the psychological ("What if we do this, and he knows it's me, and thinks I'm doing it because I like him?") to the political ("Now, can we actually get in trouble for this if we get caught?")

Game plans were put in place for every contingency. On the surface, we considered the whole idea to be a harmless, comedic, "who needs you, anyway?" Deeper ran the currents of true revenge. Tito and LBJ were, whether they knew it or not, trying to give me a leg up. We were attempting to Reverse the Whip, before we even understood what that meant. We enrolled my best friend Julie, an unparalleled scholar and extremely upstanding citizen, to round out the foursome, and went about making the final preparations.

I swear, if I go into all the details about that night, I would give myself carpal tunnel. Let me try to put a fine point on it, while still painting the word picture.

We set out late in the evening to the local grocery store to buy supplies. Now, I mentioned we were in ninth grade, right? So, how did we get there, you ask? Ahem. As the statute of limitations has run out, I can tell you. My parents drove us.

Oh, yes. They waited patiently as we bought huge armloads of bathroom tissue, and one box of cheap maxi pads. We piled them in the trunk of the car, and headed to the site.

My mother and father seemed, at a glance, like law-abiding individuals. After all, these were the people who had before, and would thereafter, give me the strictest curfew of anybody in town. Many threats were often made about the consequences of bad behavior or hanging out with the wrong people. Despite their desire that I would grow up and become a good and successful person and not some wildchild who looked for trouble wherever I could find it, my triumph over bad self-esteem was more important than some silly city ordinances. Plus, both of the Lowes had spent many years prior to my birth as crazy people. They had a lot of experience with this kind of thing. It was time for me to inherit their legacy of passive-aggressive crime and protest. As a matter of fact, in 1970, Mother, Daddy and their friends Dennis and Pat drove around Atlanta stealing Christmas trees and decorations out of office buildings. That ain't right at all. I am not sure they had any reason to do it, other than what was probably extreme intoxication, and a combined love for strange behavior. I'm just saying, they were probably prepared for the day I would be ready for the mission I had just accepted. I don't even remember my friends and I worrying about how we were going to pull this thing off, which means there was simply never any question about transport. My parents drove us to the store, to the scene of the crime, and circled the block until we were ready to make our getaway.

And they did it four years in a row. Yeah, we rolled his yard every year. We never got caught. After that first night, when we lit up the sky with ribbons of flying tissue, and Julie spelled his name out with huge white sanitary napkins in his driveway (his name was short, so she just randomly stuck the extras to trees—it was like performance art), I was so over that guy that his emotional offenses became irrelevant to me. My father got up at dawn, by himself, to drive over to Matt's house again and take pictures of the yard as the sun came up. When I look at the pictures today, the beauty of the whole thing still blinds me with tears.

I can't really give you any more details about that and other events in the years that followed. We're talking secret society here, OK? I'd have to kill you. I've said too much already. When I got my wedding pictures back (before they burned[1]), I was happy to see that Tito had paid tribute to our past history by sticking her bridesmaid bouquet into a roll of toilet paper and forcing the photographer to take a picture of it. It is gorgeous.

---

1. The author and her husband lost their home and their dog, Murphy, in a fire in May 2003.

As I have grown up and entered into and out of relationships, I try not to tell any of the stories about this particular group of my friends until a level of real trust has been reached. I don't want to have to break up with somebody for sneering at our bonds of love and evil or making light of our rituals. Only we can do that. Conversely, I don't want anyone to be scared off when they learn about our techniques of Non-Violent Getting Even With the World. Chris[2] has been both fascinated and repelled by our thirst for justice and, sometimes, harmless petty thievery, and has chosen not to even discuss any activity that could harm his reputation or make him an accessory. I respect his position, I guess, but he's probably going to have to end up getting over it.

(The thing is, ALL of us married guys like this. How? Tito's husband? We call him The Poodle because of his yippy nerves. LBJ married the most stand-up character serving his country today. The Bean is now Mrs. Dr. Radiologist. That guy just wants to look at X-rays and fly fish the rest of his life. They all prefer to be peaceful. Julie remains our only unmarried compatriot and thus our only hope. All of these so-called "men" are too afraid to be getaway drivers.)

I think Chris is at least tolerant of my dark attitudes, because he's from Jersey and is familiar with the mafia. His is a respectful fear. For example, he fully supported my plot to design the most ridiculous bulletin board my office has ever imagined, and comforted me when it backfired and my coworkers ended up loving it. (Sigh. That is an entirely separate entry—I am sure you will appreciate it when I say it made me even more angry about doing the bulletin board when I based it on a theme of baked beans and hitchhiking and OJ Simpson's birthday and everybody thought it was "neat." I got even more bizarre for the August version, and though I did get a few worried glances, it was still a huge hit. I don't understand people.)

I haven't had to roll anyone's yard in a long time, but that's not to say the passion has died out, nor does it mean I'll never have to do it again. Since the fire, I have been scheming endlessly about making a fairly harmless strike against our former landlords, on whose shoulders, rightly or wrongly, I place full blame for the obliteration of our worldly possessions and our dog and the near-ruination of our lives. What I really want to do is set up some kind of memorial to Murphy. Something really annoying, but not harmful to the environment. It would have to be something at least mildly destructive, as no tribute to that dog could ever be anything else. If you

---

2. The author's husband

think of any ideas, let me know. However, Chris will have no part in it. That's fine. I've already got people lined up to come get me from jail.

Since my gang of high school associates (sure, we have an official name, but I can't reveal it) now all live far away, I am sometimes lonely in my plans for retribution against the various forces in the world designed to get me down. However, hope is dawning in the form of some as-yet-unknown trashy neighbor of ours in the Beige Box Village.

The team who "manages" our apartments—complete with a girl named Summer, who talks so loud you wouldn't believe it—has deemed it necessary to install a gated security system equal in obesity and effectiveness to that of the system at your local international airport. Meaning, you can see why such measures would be necessary, but they are so ridiculously inefficient you feel less secure having them in place. There are huge iron gates that open when you pull up to use your secret electronic key card. Those take long enough to open, but when they finally do, you have to wait another full minute for the wooden drop bar in front of them to rise up and let you into the complex. Why? When I finally make it home in the afternoons, I just want to park and run inside. Anybody robbing the joint could simply climb over the dumb gate, anyway. I mean, I don't want any of our five post-fire possessions to get stolen, certainly, so the iron gate is fine as a deterrent, and I don't mind waiting for it to open. It's the drop bar that is so maddening. There are three gates, one entrance for people who live there, one entrance for people who don't, and one exit gate. They all have drop bars.

I know they've put them in place to keep people from sneaking in behind residents as they drive through the gates, but 90 percent of the time, they don't work anyway. And, why the one on the exit? They don't want anybody rushing out?

The things drive me CRAZY. And, apparently, I'm not alone, because someone keeps breaking them. Every single day, one or all of them is broken and thrown in the bushes, leaving only a jagged shard of wood behind. I don't know when they do it, or how they keep getting away with it, but I am behind them all the way. It's a huge scandal among the divorcees and single parents who represent our neighbors in Beige Box Village. Chris calls it "Gategate."

I think he is secretly afraid it's me who's doing it, but I would never cause expensive damage like that. I just find it heartening that someone is trying to stick it to The Man in this mildly subversive way. I like to imagine it's someone who lives there who has been screwed over by the management. I daydream that he broods, much like me about my teenaged broken heart or my burned down house or my office bulletin board, lying in wait in the dark, thinking, "OK, Summer. You won't install overhead lights in my apartment? That's fine. If I must live in this place and sit on this balcony overlooking the parking lot, I'll just have to find some way to get even, in some small way... with the ENTIRE WORLD."

So, when all is quiet, he sneaks down in the dark and bends those wooden barriers until the break. Walking back to his dark apartment, he must feel so satisfied. I hope so, anyway. It's the most brilliant whip reversal since yard rolling. All that comeuppance delivered, and he can just stroll leisurely back to bed. And, though I would most certainly volunteer for the job, he doesn't even need a getaway driver.

Site: Hate Your Daddy

URL: http://hateyourdaddy.com/

Customers I Have Driven Out Of The Store

Ali Davis

If you don't count rousting teenagers out of the porn section, I have only driven away two and a half customers.

The only one I'm proud of happened pretty recently. I was ringing up a sale and I heard a crash from downstairs. My manager was out, so I couldn't leave the register to go down and see what happened. I glanced at the security monitor and saw a guy downstairs calmly flipping through the DVD section. He had knocked down three entire shelves. Instead of picking them up or coming to get me or even shoving them over into a pile and then continuing his porn shopping, he was just standing in them and on them, flipping away.

I got on the Voice of God microphone and said, in as friendly a voice as I could, "Hi! Could you pick those up, please?"

He started, then came charging up the stairs.

> "It was an accident!" he yelled, "Knocking over those DVDs was an accident!"
>
> "I believe you, sir." I said.
>
> "And you want me to pick them up? You want ME to pick them up?!"

And without waiting for an answer, he stormed out.

Actually, I didn't really expect him to pick them up. I wouldn't have minded picking them up if he'd just come upstairs and said something like "Jesus, I'm an idiot and I knocked down a substantial chunk of your DVD section." Or put them into halfhearted little piles. Or really anything other than just standing on them while continuing to shop for porn.

I don't think he was as angry at the notion that he might have to clean up his own mess so much as he was furious that he'd been caught making it. Sometimes new customers don't see the security cameras right away, and they sure as hell don't expect the Voice of God mike. When you're scrutinizing the charming cover art of "White Trash Whore" the last thing you want is to be chastised by a booming voice from above.

I'm not particularly sorry we lost his business. I do feel bad about driving away Mr. Creaky, even though he used to give me the creeps. Mr. Creaky was not, technically, a porn customer. He liked the Japanese animation. The Anime section is the one that really makes me cringe. It's upstairs in the general releases since it's all, you know, cartoons, and some of it is charming fare like "My Neighbor Totoro." But a lot of it is incredibly hardcore stuff—way worse than we'll allow in the real-people porn downstairs.

My position on porn is that I'm fine with whatever floats your boat, as long as everyone involved is a consenting adult. Manga throws both of those rules out the window. Sure, all the boxes claim that all the characters are at least 18, but a lot of them are clearly drawn to look about 12. And there's a lot of raping. Not just run-of-the-mill raping, either—we're talking about triple-penetration rape by demons.

I consider myself a first-amendment feminist, but to be honest the anime section really makes me wrestle with that sometimes. And guys that rent the entire "La Blue Girl" series all at once (check out the box cover sometimes and you'll see what I mean) freak me out even worse than the guys who rent the "Animal Trainer" series.[3]

We have to watch the anime section because it's right next to the foreign films and the tags are the same color, which means a clerk who isn't on his toes could check out a shitload of hardcore animated underage rape porn to a kid and yes, once they see that there's sex stuff on some of the boxes kids definitely try to slide it past.

Mr. Creaky, as you've guessed, was hardly a kid. I would have been frightened of him if he hadn't been so old and feeble. He would rent a stack of rape manga at least once a week. He always had the same patter as he came up to the register: "Do you watch that show The Sopranos?"

"No, sir."

"I hear it's pretty good."

"Yes, sir, that's what I hear too."

"I'd like to watch that show, but I can't. There's too much cussing."

Then, clever ruse in place, he would bring up his tags for "Demon Beast."

Anyway, all would have been well had it not been for a well-meaning but plateheaded clerk name Dan. Dan was a sweetheart, but had an astonishing ability to fuck things up. In this case Dan had rented six of our very foulest titles to a 16-year-old. To give you the idea of the level of stupidity this involves, I'll just go ahead and tell you that the "La Blue Girl" tapes depict a woman being raped by demons RIGHT ON THE BOX. I was horrified both at the

3. No, we don't carry bestiality. "Animal Trainer" is about training women.

thought of what this kid's mom would do to us when she found out and what this kid had just learned about the beautiful, tender world of lovemaking.

I talked to my manager. We didn't want to move the whole anime section so we needed a bright, easy signal for Dan who for some reason still hadn't been fired yet. Our solution was to let the R-rated stuff slide, but if anything looked more like an X I highlighted the label on the tag and wrote a big "NC-17" on it.[4]

Mr. Creaky never came back.

So how did I manage to drive away half a customer? Well, he's not really quite gone yet. He still comes into the store a lot, but I may have destroyed his soul.

Mr. Buddy was the first guy people warned me about when I started working at the store. He is heavily addicted to porn and a huge pain in the ass. He also desperately wants to be friends with the clerks. He wants to come behind the counter and look at the boxes when new porn comes in. We always tell him that customers can't come behind the counter and he says "Yeah, but I can, right?" No, he can't. Sometimes with a new clerk he'll try "The old manager used to let me come behind the counter," at which point any other employee in earshot will chime in with "No, he didn't."

He bitches about the prices and tries to haggle with us. "I swear to you, this has been on the new release shelf for a long time. I should get it for the old release price, right?" Wrong. One time he brought back just a case, without the DVD in it. He actually expected me to check the empty case in and let him, you know, just drop the DVD by at his convenience. When I said no, he stood at the register and whined for nearly ten minutes.

His bitching and wheedling isn't caused so much by the fact that he's a cheapskate, which he is, as by the fact that he desperately wants to be a regular. He wants to be greeted by name and not have to show ID and get whatever mythical special privileges he's imagining. The problem, of course, is that we're the ones who decide if he's a regular or not, and we don't like him.

The fact that he's an asshole is part of the problem, and the other part is that he seems to be completely devoid of social skills. Even the total dirtbags know better than to hit on me when I'm putting tags away downstairs. Mr. Buddy did not.

---

4. Yes, this is a violation of MPAA copyright.

And again, he desperately, desperately wants to be friends with us. He's maybe 45 years old, and has a good enough job to spend literally thousands of dollars a year on porn alone. We can't figure out why he wants to be friends so badly, but he does. "You guys are awesome!" he'll say after trying to get Dustin to pay the extra $.50 he owes for him, "Seriously, you guys are the best!" Never, not once, has he received a positive response to this behavior, but he still does it. "You guys rule, you know that?" I've met Golden Retriever puppies with more dignity.

I always try to be civil to him in a distant, customer service sort of way, which is apparently the best he gets.

("You're always so nice to me! You rule!")

Round about September 14th he brought in a picture he'd downloaded from the internet. It was President Bush photoshopped so that he had a long beard and was dressed in vaguely Middle Eastern clothes. Mr. Buddy had drawn a cartoon voice balloon coming out of his mouth so that he was saying, "Rent at [My Store's Name] Video!"

I wasn't offended so much by any sort of tastelessness as I was by the completely failed attempt at humor. There wasn't even a vestigal joke. He handed it to me, and I made the same noncommital noise you make when you've been handed a drawing by a small child and then tried to hand it back. "No," he said, "I made it for you guys! You keep it!" So I kept it until he left, then threw it away. The next time Mr. Buddy came in he was all upset—he'd actually expected us to post it behind the register.

You wouldn't think it would be possible to drive away Mr. Buddy, but it turns out you can. As I said, I have always been civil with him, even when he is making yet another attempt to get me to waive his late fees. But a couple of weeks ago he caught me at the end of a heavy dirtball day. We'd been swamped—pervs, box thieves, scam artists, people dropping tapes and running without paying for them, and plenty of general crabbiness. And it was a new porn day, so the phone had been ringing off the hook and I just wanted to get the hell out of there. I was very, very tired. Mr. Buddy was one of my last customers. He pulled his usual fucking routine for about five minutes, then as I started checking out his tapes launched into how awesome we were.

I don't remember the exact phrasing of what was said. I just remember that one of the other clerks made a joke about closing early or closing altogether, and Mr. Buddy said something like "Aw, you can't do that—I need you guys! Who am I gonna hang out with?"

“Oh, Jesus, don’t say that!” I said, “We can’t be your only source of emotional support!” I tried to turn my voice up into a joke at the last second, which almost worked.

“Don’t say that,” Mr. Buddy tried to joke back, “You make me sound pathetic.”

We made eye contact before I could compose my face. In that moment, Mr. Buddy knew that I do, in fact, find him pathetic. And I’m the nice one. He still comes in, but he isn’t chatty anymore. The other clerks love it. I feel like a creep.

Site: True Porn Clerk Stories

URL: http://improvisation.ws/mb/showthread.php?s=&threadid=4475

Interview with Ali Davis of True Porn Clerk Stories

At minimum wage, writer and improv performance artist Ali Davis found herself in a job where men shared their inner most desires, nervous ticks and unfortunately, a few body fluids. Davis was living the strange existence as a porn store clerk, and to stay sane she kept a blog documenting her day-to-day work life.

In the beginning her obscure blog was merely read by friends and their friends. But soon word spread and "True Porn Clerk Stories" became a regular pit stop for strangers who were curious about her adventures in dealing with creepy characters and sticky store shelves.

Currently, Davis is writing two screenplays, one of which is based on the porn clerk journal and one that has nothing to do with sex at all. She continues to perform with Baby Wants Candy, her improv group back in Chicago, and is starting to explore the improv scene in her new home of Los Angeles.

Working as a porn video clerk is a job most people haven't had to experience. What are some of the weirder job elements you've written about in your blog?

Well, the daily hazard of getting semen on my hands seems to have been an attention-grabber.

Actually, that marrow-chilling experience—no one ever got used to it—sort of sums up a lot about what was interesting about clerking. To do my job well, I had to be politely detached, but I was dealing with incredibly personal, primal urges with a lot of my customers. I'd see a person for the first time in my life, then ten seconds later just from scanning in his stack of videos I'd know what his deepest kink was. The combination of incredible intimacy and personal removal was always fascinating to me.

Some of the porn really bothered me at first, and not always for good reasons. I chewed on that a lot and I learned some things about myself that were interesting to me, if not anyone else. When something bothered me on a knee-jerk level but my brain couldn't find a reason why, I had to rethink and readjust. It wasn't always easy and I wasn't always successful, but the process was interesting and made me think a lot about tolerance and where my ethical boundaries are. I don't think most people think about whether pregnancy porn or *bukkake* is inherently wrong—I certainly didn't until I started clerking—but when it's right there in your face, you have to.

Why did you feel compelled to write about your experiences online?

I honestly had no idea the journal would take off the way it did. I'm an improviser, and my friend Kevin Mullaney runs the Improv Resource Center message board. It's a small (and friendly) community and I either knew or felt like I knew pretty much everyone who was on the boards at the time. At what I thought would be the journal's height, there were maybe 75 people who'd check it out regularly, all of whom were either friends or people who were just a degree of separation or two away. I can't tell you what specific incident made me start posting. Kevin had started a journals section a few months earlier and one night I came home after a rough shift with a deep need to blow off steam. It became a good way to process what was going in my head in a format that forced me to be coherent, with an ending and a beginning and a point just in case someone actually read it.

On a side note, once the link started getting passed around, the Improv Resource Center boards got swamped with visitors. Many of the new arrivals became great new additions to the community, but unfortunately a lot of them just started barging around the place without even bothering to find out what the boards were about. If people do stop by the site to check out the whole journal, I'd like to ask that they take the time to get a feel for the site and find out about the community, think a bit before posting, and be polite to their hosts. Thanks.

What has the reaction been from people regarding your blog? What did you learn from the experience?

I've had reactions across the board. The vast majority of the people who've bothered to drop me a note have been a normal level of friendly, and I'm very grateful for that. I really enjoy those e-mails—it's pretty cool to have a stranger drop into my life just long enough to say hi or that he or she enjoyed my writing and then drop right back out again.

A few people proposed marriage, with varying degrees of seriousness. The one who said he did well enough at his computer job that I could just hang out and write all day was pretty tempting, but I'm pretty sure he was kidding.

And then there were many people who really, really hated me. Total strangers called me a huge bitch, and anti-porn feminists (yes, there are other kinds) wrote me long, angry e-mails because I don't think porn is inherently evil. I got absolutely torn apart on the Ms. message boards. But, hey, if I can soak up the praise from strangers I should also be able to take the criticism.

A few Chicagoans thought they recognized my store from the descriptions and began little games of Find the Porn Clerk. I'm pretty sure it was all in fun, but it was a little disturbing to be found.

The weirdest responses I got were maybe 7 or 8 e-mails, all from people who identified themselves as men, most of them middle-aged. For some reason they were compelled to write me long, long e-mails about what kind of porn they liked and why. And what porn meant to them and what they thought about sex and women and relationships and on and on...I cannot stress enough how long these e-mails were. I'm still not sure what was going on with these guys—after the first couple I'd just skim enough to see that, yeah, it was another one of those e-mails and I'd delete it.

I think these men were just so happy to have found a woman who didn't completely condemn porn that they felt like maybe they could tell me everything. Which wasn't a bad impulse, but it was a misguided one. To be honest, I don't think I made it all the way through even one of them—reading those things was the last thing I wanted do after a full day of dishing out porn at the video store. I felt sort of bad about not responding, but I knew writing them back wouldn't be a good idea. Just the thought of it was emotionally exhausting.

One guy who I lump into this category wanted to have an extended e-mail debate and said that we had much to talk about and that I clearly hated all straight, white men. Then he stressed that I should NOT try to trace his e-mail address because he was so famous and rich and powerful and had so much to lose, and besides, he had too thoroughly encrypted it for me to succeed anyway. I declined.

The lesson I learned most thoroughly from my responses was that people who hold a given point of view too passionately are not, as a rule, careful readers. They pretty much see what they go in expecting to see, no matter what's actually there. Both the people who frothed at me for not saying that all pornography is wonderful and the people who frothed at me for not saying that all pornography is evil tended to accuse me of writing things I hadn't and to take little out-of-context chunks of text and wildly distort their meanings. I think soothing music and deep breathing exercises could do a lot for the state of intelligent debate in this country.

The best lesson I learned was that people in general are pretty cool. I was astonished at how many people bothered to drop friendly notes to a complete stranger. It was very heartening to get tangible proof that, yeah, the vast majority of people are just good people.

What do you hope people learn about you from your writing?

I'm always glad when people say they've gotten something out of the journal, regardless of what it is. If I'm trying to be humble I say it's rewarding, but I think I really like it because it's flattering.

If there's one main thing I'd like people to bring away, it's BE NICE TO YOUR VIDEO CLERK!

Why do you think blogging has become so popular in the last few years?

Well, it's masturbatory. You get to say what you think for as long as you want without all that tedious conversational back-and-forth. And then maybe it'll turn out someone was watching you the whole time and he or she will tell you you're fabulous.

Oh, I don't really mean that.

There's a practical reason for keeping an online journal that I've never seen mentioned: my handwriting sucks. I've kept much more personal paper journals off and on, and honestly the only element that really turns me off of them is that I finish writing and look at the beautiful page in this beautiful leather-bound little thing I've spent too much money on and there I've gone and absolutely wrecked it with my terrible handwriting. There's a sequence at the beginning of "1984" where Winston does the same thing and I remember reading it in sixth or seventh grade and thinking "Yes, Mr. Orwell, YES! I'M RIGHT HERE WITH YOU!"

(On the upside, I never worry about people finding and reading my journals because they all look like they've been written in Linear B.) So the speed and ease of typing and editing and seeing a good-looking finished product may be a minor factor in how so many blogs got going.

But I think the really great thing about blogs is that for the first time we have a true freedom of the press and people are running with it. Anyone with access to a computer can start publishing and that's exhilarating. I loved it that the mainstream press didn't pick up on Trent Lott's comments about how the U.S. would be a better place if segregationist Strom Thurmond had become President until a few bloggers started crying foul and forced them to take notice. I love it that there is passionate political thought and argument everywhere that isn't being filtered by a few big media conglomerations. And for all my own swiping at the masturbatory nature of blogs, I do love it that people talk about themselves. I think the biggest cause of intolerance is ignorance—most people who say they hate gay people, for example, think they've never met one. This is a way to meet each other. The more opportunities we have to read about and understand each other, the better the world is going to get.

And, what the hell, they're fun.

Never Threaten to Eat Your Co-Workers

Uncle Bob

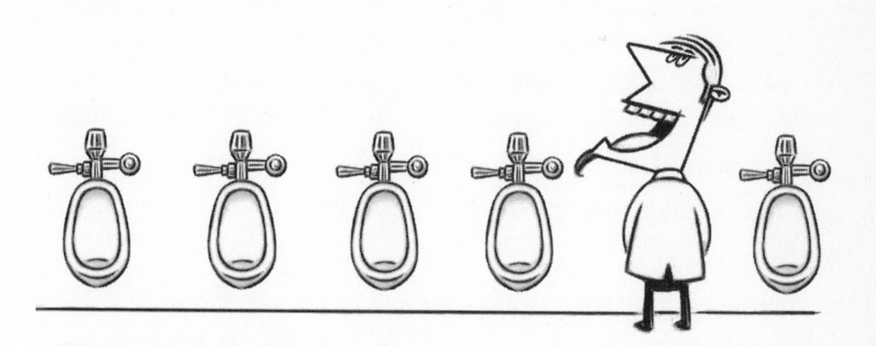

So yesterday I'm driving to work, listening to Radiohead's "Hail To The Thief." And the song playing is a song called "Where I End And You Begin." I think it's a song about sex, myself. Where the sweaty genitalia meet. Yeah. That's what I believe all right.

So near the end of the song, Thom Yorke (lead singer and professional imp) is saying the line "I will eat you alive" over and over again. It's really kind of cool because you can't really distinguish what he's saying at first and then at the end it's clear as a bell.

Seriously. Stick with me here. So I get out of my car as that song is ending. And as normal, I'm singing the song as I walk into the building. More to the point...I'm saying, "I will eat you alive" over and over again.

I get in the building, nobody's around and I'm just...you know..."I will eat you alive, I will eat you alive, I will eat you alive."

I decide that before I go to my desk, I shall take a whiz. I go in the main bathroom. A big bathroom. Three toilet stalls, three urinals, two sinks. Good sized bathroom. Keep in mind...I'm the only guy in the building at this point.

I go in, still singing/saying this phrase. The acoustics in the bathroom are phenomenal. So I kick it up a notch while I pee.

"I WILL EAT YOU ALIVE! I WILL EAT YOU ALIVE! I WILL EAT YOU ALIVE!"

...Really getting into it at this point. All of a sudden, I hear a toilet flush.

I never saw who it was. They hauled ASS outta there scared shitless that Hannibal Lechter had somehow escaped from prison and was crooning their death march to them as they were "dropping the kids off at the pool" if'n you know what I mean.

Of course, for a few seconds, I was faced with the dilemma of immediately stopping the singing or continuing like I was confident in myself and had no problem singing threatening lyrics in bathrooms to men taking a dump. I continued on for the five seconds the guy stayed in the bathroom with me.

I'm still wondering who it was. Hopefully, he has no idea it was me.

And we can just quietly forget this ever happened.

****

Everyone had gone to lunch, leaving me and Wendigo in the office.

Now, for months, I've had this stuff called Slush Powder in my desk drawer. When you sprinkle this powder in a glass of water, it automatically turns the water into gel. Takes like 10 seconds to do. It's really kinda amazing. Magicians use it, but it also makes for a great practical joke. Which is why I own it.

So everyone's at lunch, I'm manning the phone system and I think to myself, "I wonder if anyone left a glass of water on their desks?" Sure enough...two women had done just that. I get my Slush Powder and I sprinkle some in there. Both glasses of water are now filled with a sponge-y solid mass. About an hour passes and one of the women comes back from lunch.

She starts saying, "What happened to my water??"

Now, I'm not the best at keeping a straight face in these types of situations. But I have to admit, I did pretty well. Because every time I was about to crack up, I made an "Ewwwww!" face instead.

This woman went on for 10-15 minutes about her water. Everyone started coming back from lunch and was crowded around her cup, speculating on what the hell had happened. She filled up another cup of water and put it on her desk, leaving it there to see if the same thing would happen to that water. While she's doing all this, I went to lunch with a couple of girls from the office. We're gone an hour...hour and 15 minutes.

While we're gone, Water Woman has contacted our parent corporation up the street who are nice people, but rather humorless. They are very disturbed by this and want to have the water tested. In the meantime, NOBODY is allowed to drink water from our water cooler. A sample of the gelled water is sent to them and is sitting on the desk of the President of the organization.

They believe there's something either toxic in the water or the cups. But they're putting in calls to the EPA to get to the bottom of this.

Meanwhile, I'm in a bistro, eating a burger and fries and not thinking anything about this little prank.

We get back from lunch and Water Woman is convinced it's something in the cups because while we were gone, they discovered that the other woman who's cup I tainted...well by God...IT HAPPENED TO HER TOO!!!

So I go to my office, get the Slush Powder out of my drawer, walk up to where all the hubbub is going on and say, "It very well could be the cups causing this...but there's a chance it could be this Slush Powder as well."

Everyone gets a chuckle and admits it was a good prank and had everyone fooled and ah ha ha ha ha.

Then, the President of the organization gets wind of this. And he wants to talk to my boss. And I'm told that I'm on thin ice. And everyone is coming to my office telling me I'm on thin ice. And yet they're all trying not to smile as they say this. And they're saying the President, whom I barely know, hasn't got patience for things like this because we are a very professional organization.

And meanwhile some guy is frantically running around the building trying to find out who was threatening to eat him alive in the bathroom that morning.

And my life just completely sucks.

Site: Uncle Bob!

URL: http://unclebob.diaryland.com/

Interview with Uncle Bob

Writer Uncle Bob works in the tour industry for Alabama. But it's not his job that gets people to read his blog, it's the incidents that occur at his job. In addition to his blog and various freelance writing, Uncle Bob has crafted scripts for television shows and commercials, and written over a dozen published books under his real name. Always drawn to creative endeavors, Uncle Bob worked as a stand-up comedian and then a successful disc jockey.

Why did you feel compelled to write about your experiences online?

Originally, I started writing online while I was also writing a humor column for the local newspaper. This journal was basically used as a springboard to try new ideas and jokes for the newspaper column. If I received positive feedback from certain entries, I'd incorporate those into my columns. Plus, it gave me an outlet where I could remain anonymous and write about subjects in a more "R-rated" style.

What has the reaction been from people regarding your blog? What's been the reaction from any co-workers?

I'd say the majority of response has been positive, but I've gotten my share of negative response from people as well. I like to push buttons and some entries are written just to get different reactions from people. If I make someone angry or cry or laugh or think, then I feel I've done my job as an online journalist.

Only a bare minimum of people in my real life know about Uncle Bob—basically my wife and a handful of friends. My wife has only read one entry and that was an entry about all the female friends I wished I had slept with while I had the chance. Yeah, *that* makes for interesting dinner conversation every night for the next several months, let me tell ya.

What did you learn from the experience?

People will read anything if you give it to them in short, concise bursts and occasionally drop the F-bomb.

What do you hope people learn about you from your writing?

That we should all love one another and try to live together in harmony. And if that fails, we should make fun of each other mercilessly, especially those less fortunate than us, in order to feel good about ourselves.

Brad Pitt: Your Remakes Are Ready

Stephen and Alistair Reid

For some reason while watching the first twenty minutes of "Meet Joe Black" over the weekend (Al was right, it is only worth watching to see Brad getting car-bounced all over the road like a rubber bowling pin) Al said:

"Brad Pitt should just remake every movie Robert Redford ever made."

And a light bulb went off over my head.

Let's be honest, the good ship Brad is running aground these days. Last movie he made? "Sinbad," which while I enjoyed, didn't even have his face in it. Before that? A cameo in buddy Clooney's "Confessions of a Dangerous Mind." Before that? Well to be honest it's "Ocean's Eleven"—two years ago and, let's face it, not exactly a starring vehicle for pretty boy Brad.

Next year he's got "Troy" (or The Trojan War, depends on who you listen to) coming up, which should renew his matinee idol status for a while longer. But frankly, what the boy needs is a string of decent flicks, all starring him. What he needs is Robert Redford's career, from 1969 to 1976.

"Butch Cassidy and the Sundance Kid would have to be first," I said to Al, "but we need a Newman." Think about it: Westerns are always commercial if they're done right, and even back in 69, Butch & Sundance never felt like commercial Western heroes. The trick would be not to cover up the story in a bunch of big stunt pieces. Oh, and you'd need to really work hard on persuading William Goldman to let someone re-write his script. Or you'd just pay him to re-write it himself...he's good at that re-write shit. As for our new Newman? I thought about it for a few days, and came back with George Clooney. I honestly don't think we'd do better. But feel free to disagree.

"Jeremiah Johnson," Al continued, and I had to agree. It's a little known movie that's been a favourite of mine for years, ever after I caught it on TV. Quintessentially 70s, bleak but beautiful, it's the story of a "mountain man" who finds happiness with an Indian wife, and then because it's a 70s flick, loses it and goes on a bloody vendetta.

It's like a lost Clint Eastwood western, with long, lingering camera shots, plenty of sequences with little to no dialogue, and a fantastic performance by Redford—who gets to go from laconic to ecstactic to psychotic in the course of one movie. And wear a lot of fur. While I can't see Brad taking this on without a bit of trepidation, the fact is he's grown the beard for it before—something that caused Al to speculate about this remake before. If we're really lucky, we'll get someone like Christina Aguilera to play Brad's Indian wife before she's brutally slaughtered.

"Three Days of the Condor," was the next thing that popped in my mind, although arguably Matt Damon's beat Pitt to this with *The Bourne Identity*, which has a similar man-on-the-run feel. Faye Dunaway's in this one, with Sydney Pollack directing again—a man Brad should hook up with considering he made some of Redford's best films. It's all about a CIA researcher who comes back from lunch to find that everyone in his office has been killed...and now they want him dead to finish the job. How's that for a hook huh? Get a gritty, urban director to do it (Joe Carnahan, how are you set after M:I-3?), try not to make *Enemy of the State* again and boom! I can see this.

"The Sting," was the next thing that popped into my mind, as by this point Al had wandered off to write something about *Alien*. Brad could play Redford's Johnny Hooker with his eyes shut—it's all wounded bravado and snappy dressing—and if you could get David Mamet to come in and do the screenplay (he likes the 1930s, he likes con games—who is a better fit?) and persuade Clooney to do Newman's role again, I think we're a lock. Only problem: The Entertainer ain't exactly the kind of thing that sells tie-in soundtrack CDs these days.

Last few Redford remakes Mr Pitt would do well: obviously *The Candidat*e would be easy, as it's about a political puppet running for office, but then Tim Robbins has done that awfully well already; *The Way We Were* is a lock, but then you need to find someone who could be as spunky, yet strangely attractive as Barbra is in that flick—I mean, even with that nose and those dresses.

Finally the Redford flick I think deserves to not only be remade but also updated, but couldn't be made until history gets declassified—at which point Brad might be too old to play the role—is some sort of *All the President's Men* for the early 00s.

When the truth finally comes out and the Elephant is once again run out of office, perhaps then another Woodward & Bernstein will come forward to tell the inside truth about what happened in the last three years in our Western world, and perhaps then Brad will be available to play the blonde haired, blue-eyed version of what will surely be some pasty-faced blogger with the right contacts inside Washington who finally busts the whole shithouse open.

Site: Tagline: A Movie Weblog

URL: http://www.tagliners.org

Kookoo for Coconuts

Carla Sinclair

Mark's obsession with ukuleles has been replaced by a fascination with coconuts. It's all he talks about lately. His goal today is to make coconut cream, which he will then use to make coconut chicken, creamy pasta sauce and scones from scratch.

He recruited Sarina to help him in his mission. They collected fallen coconuts this morning, spotting a few next to our laundry lines, and a couple more scattered around the border of our lawn.

Now Mark and Sarina are out in the front yard, trying to open the fruits, which is no simple matter. The edible part of a coconut is encapsulated by a fibrous shell, which is protected by another, thicker shell that—as Mark has learned—cannot be penetrated by whacking it with a sharp rock.

While Mark pries the outer shells open with his handmade ironwood spear (which took him two days to carve and sharpen), Sarina sits on the grass with a bush knife in hand, whacking the inner shells in half.

"You could slice off someone's head with one of those knives," I hear Mark say.

"Really?" Sarina squeals.

I flinch as she raises the knife up into the air, and wonder if I should interfere. I don't think a bush knife, which must be in the same family as a machete, is an age-appropriate tool for a 6-year-old. But then she cracks the coconut open, a perfect split, and she and Mark hoot with delight.

Once the coconuts are all opened, the white "meat" needs to be grated. Again, this is no simple matter. It's not something you can do with your ordinary cheese grater. The fruit is tenaciously tough and must be shredded with a coconut scraper. After days of looking in shops for a scraper, which everyone on the island seems to own, Mark found out that no one sells these tools. They are handmade by bolting a section of a car's leaf spring onto a small wooden bench.

Until Mark is able to rig together one of his own, he'll be borrowing our landlord's scraper.

Mark and Sarina argue over who gets to scrape the coconuts, and Sarina wins. She straddles the bench with half a coconut in hand, bends forward, and begins to scrape the inside of the shell against the metal scraper. The moist shreds fall into a bucket. She stops for a moment to peel off her shirt; then continues to grate until she runs out of coconuts.

Mark scoops the white mush into a large piece of cheesecloth and wrings it into a jar, which also contains fresh clear milk from the coconuts. It's surprising how much liquid squirts out of the cloth.

He's now ready to begin cooking.

Jane is napping, so I decide to steal Sarina for the afternoon. We head down to the beach and rent a bright-orange kayak. The boat has an inch of water that sloshes around our feet as we paddle out to a motu, or islet. The bottom of the shallow lagoon is patched with huge black spots, which, we soon find out, are clusters of sea cucumbers. Sarina leans way over the boat, almost capsizing us.

"What are you doing?" I shout.

She laughs and holds up a fat limp cucumber, as if she'd just won a trophy.

We come home famished. Mark walks out to the front yard to greet us, looks up at our palm tree, and by sheer luck, witnesses a coconut falling from its top. It thumps to the ground with a force that could crack a skull. His eyes water with amazement, the way Moses may have wept when he witnessed the parting of the Red Sea.

I make a mental note to stay clear of that tree when hanging my clothes on the line.

Site: The Island Chronicles

URL: http://boingboing.net/island/

You've Got Ringworm

Mark Frauenfelder

In the morning I take 4-month-old Jane for a walk. She falls asleep, and I leave her stroller outside the door of the little Seventh-day Adventist groceries while I go inside for a newspaper. I notice Tia, our landlady, standing near a little table at the front of the store, looking through a stack of envelopes. (The market doubles as the village's mail depot.) We chat for a bit, and then I show her a recently developed sore on my leg. It started off as a crusty, oozing scab, but is now a quarter-size patch, angry red, surrounded by a darker ring. I ask her if she's ever seen anything like it.

She studies it with a flat expression for several seconds; then says, "What is it?"

"I don't know," I say. "I thought maybe this was something that happens a lot to people here."

Tia looks at the sore again, then turns back to the table to flip through the envelopes. "No," she says.

Something outside the market catches my eye. I turn to see three skinny, feral dogs sniffing at Jane's feet. I run over, flapping my hands at them. They skitter away, eyeing me with a mixture of fear and longing. One of the dogs limps. Though they're wild, the dogs on the island retain vestiges of domesticity. A part of them wants to hook up with humans, while another wants to run with the pack.

Later that day, as Carla, Sarina and I sit down at our dinner table to eat fresh grilled tuna steaks, papaya with coconut cream, and steamed rice, there's a knock on our door. It startles us—no one ever knocks here, besides Jehovah's Witnesses hoping to unload a copy of The Watchtower.

Through the door's bumpy textured window, I make out the shape of a stout brown-skinned woman wearing gigantic glasses. I fork a big chunk of garlicky tuna in my mouth and chew it quickly, then get up to answer the door. Tia is holding a clear plastic bag with something that looks like green tentacles in it.

"Hi," she says in her loud, clipped Rarotonga-New Zealand accent. Her smile reveals big strong teeth. "I brought you some aloe vera for your leg." She says it like she's asking a question.

Inside our house, Tia picks up a sharp knife sitting on our kitchen counter, and pulls a plump aloe vera tendril from the bag. She sits in a chair next to the dining table with her broad thighs spread apart and her bare feet planted on the tile floor. I sit in a chair facing her. Before she cuts into the plant, I point out that the knife has tuna bits on it. She picks up one of our napkins, wipes off the knife, then deftly slices and skins a chunk of aloe vera.

"Put this on your leg," she says, handing me the glistening green slice. I do, and it feels cool and soothing.

The next day, the sore is no better. In fact, it's become larger, moving right past a freckle on my leg that I'd been using as a marker to measure its rate of growth.

I drive to the pharmacy. The pharmacist barely needs to glance at it. "Ah."

She walks to a shelf and pulls down a tube of cream. "You've got ringworm. It's a fungus, not a parasite. You'll need to apply this for seven weeks after it goes away, even though the instructions say to apply it for two. The strain here is more resistant to anti-fungal medicines than it is in other places."

I immediately apply the cream to the fungus, and then think about Tia. She said she'd come and check on the sore in a few days. Although the pharmacist said I wouldn't need the aloe vera plant, it wouldn't hurt to use it along with the cream.

Site: The Island Chronicles

URL: http://boingboing.net/island/

Interview with Mark Frauenfelder and Carla Sinclair of The Island Chronicles

Ever fantasize about dropping your current hectic lifestyle and moving to a remote island paradise? Editor/illustrator Mark Frauenfelder and his wife, writer Carla Sinclair often dreamt of temporarily relocating from Los Angeles to the South Pacific. So one day, they packed up a few essential items, closed up shop and moved, with their two small children to the island of Rarotonga—a place where coconuts are more useful than cell phones.

To keep in touch with friends and family, they started Island Chronicles, a blog featuring Mark and Carla's insights about the transition to island living, accompanied by lush, and sometimes humorous photographs.

Why do you feel people might want to read about your experiences uprooting from Los Angeles to live on a remote island?

A lot of people have fantasized about living on a tropical island, so we wanted to share our experience of what it was like to actually live out the fantasy.

Have you been getting some interesting email feedback about your Island Chronicles blog?

A few people are actually planning to follow in our footsteps and go to Rarotonga with their kids. And some people think we're spoiled jerks, because they can't get it through their heads that you don't have to be a retired millionaire to live on a tropical island. We worked the whole time we were in Rarotonga. Carla and I wrote articles and I did illustrations. We had bills to pay, even in paradise!

What have you learned from your transition from city life to island life?

I learned that the buzzing mediasphere I am used to living in is just a form of entertainment, but not an important aspect of survival. While in Rarotonga, I had the world's slowest Internet connection, which was a good thing, because I focused my attention on hiking, walking, exploring, swimming, playing with my kids—things that are free and analog. I'm trying to keep this attitude back in LA. I think it's working, so far. It's easy to slip back into the always-switched-on-lifestyle though, so I have to be careful.

Why do you think blogging has become so popular in the last few years? How do you feel about the new trend of travel blogging?

One reason is that blogs are easier to keep fresh than plain old home pages, so people are more likely to update them. This makes it more likely that other people will visit. This cycle feeds on itself.

I love the way bloggers sniff out the truth and get to the bottom of stories faster than mainstream media. I know a lot of reporters use blogs as a source of story ideas.

Lost In Translation

Greg Howard

My first few days at college, I didn't know a soul so I wandered into the dorm lobby and hung out by the pool table. Eventually I started playing with an asian student. Eventually I met his friends, and 15 years later three of us are still close friends who live and work in northern california. One of them is getting married in December, which means I now know his fiancee and her friends and her family. Yesterday, at a restaurant to sample the food that'll be served at the wedding banquet, I stood out as the lone caucasian at a table of chinese and filipino guests. From a blurry distance, I probably looked like a marshmallow floating on top of a sea of butterscotch.

My friends obviously speak English but their parents' skills tend to be dicier. The nice thing is, the parents will talk to you anyway. It doesn't matter whether you understand them or they understand you. The bride-to-be's mother turns to me and says something that sounds like:

"Konichiwa don how?"

I respond:

"I definitely have a problem with steel tariffs even if the short-term impact is to the protect the working class."

"Yes, yes! Konichia don how."

And we can go on like this for several minutes and end happily by drinking tea. The point is to be social, even if the exchange of information is highly limited.

The food tasting itself was also educational. I eat chinese food frequently, but this was serious banquet food and it carried its own set of unique traditions. I learned to watch everyone else before helping myself to the next course. Otherwise, I'd get involved in a conversation like:

"You like those kneecaps of braised duck?"

"Oh yes, delicious—"

"NO NO, do not throw bones away!"

"Oh. What do I do with them?"

"You take the bones and you hurl them at the other members of the wedding party. The flailing of poultry parts reminds us that every beginning also has an ending."

Site: Geese Aplenty

URL: http://greghoward.net/weblog

A Smart Suit And A Kipper Tie, A Big Arrow Pointing To My Fly...

Choire Sicha

My ears are pleasantly ringing. The basement bathroom at the Roseland Ballroom in the Theater District was smoky like a hookah parlor. It's fantastic, big like a Turkish prison: the urinals are mounted on both sides of a 5-foot wall. Watching straight rocker boys pee face to face is just awesome, particularly if each and every one of them is smoking like James Dean.

Neil was kind enough to take me out to the Mars Volta show tonight. I'm always scared to meet people from online, figuring that they'll be techno-schnooks with no social skills. Neil is quite not so. He's fucking great. He reminds me of my friend Kirk in San Francisco (a Scorpio as well, hmm!), but Neil's Australian and super-spastic like myself. The spastic part; I'm really not Australian at all. Anyway, it's a different era now on the internet: real people have weblogs these days, and you meet them and there's nothing to be afraid of. Not that you/we weren't real or were scary back in the day. Except a bunch of you were. Ach. You know what I mean.

Get this: my cab broke down at 7:30 p.m. at 10th Avenue and 23rd Street on my way to meet Neil. Died in the middle of mad traffic. The driver said, oh this happens all the time and encouraged me—made me—take another cab. Easier said than done on a Friday night, but finally I hailed this minivan. Suddenly everyone impatiently waiting at the bus stop wanted to know where I was going. So a gang piled in, three odd women, strangers to each other. We were dropping the first at the Javits Convention Center. And I asked, why are you going to the Javits on a Friday night? Turns out she was going to see an evangelical healer. Right here in New York City. A Jewish fellow in fact, name of Mario...Cerulus? Something odd that we thought was Marcus Aurelius. Anyway, she'd once had a bone spur healed by an evangelist, so now she loves to go and watch the healings. The other two women and I were...astounded, and amused, and totally in love with her.

A few hours later, standing (rather sexily) ass to crotch with strangers in the psychotically loud wall-to-wall 20-year-old crowd, I realized that I've made some recent trade-offs in this life. Sure, sure, haven't we all. But I remember the immortal words of Ms. Sheryl Crow: all I want to do is have some fun. Please do remember—and few of you will—that I once literally raffled myself off as an internet visitor prize. If you like complex levels of irony, just enjoy this and leave it unremarked upon: nowadays if I leave some stupid snotty comment on someone's website, for instance, inevitably I'm called on some polyblend carpet over it. Maybe I liked it better when everyone just rolled their eyes and thought, oh, that fag again and ignored me.

Well: I'm sure most people still do. Good. I certainly do.

So is there some way I can treat the internet as my playground still, even while I dress for business every day? Or maybe this is true for everyone these days too. Maybe there's no high-spirited sleazy fun anymore. I don't want the reckless stupid era of the internet to end: I don't want this to become corporate rock. Because, as we always say, when you become like everyone else and give up who you are, you end up face down on the bottom of an empty motel swimming pool. You end up boring, and I can't afford to bore myself. Corporate rock still sucks.

And I wanna rhumba. I wanna cha-cha. I wanna play some miniature golf.

It's been nice, if a little unnerving, to write this. It's not particularly well-written, and I wouldn't dream of writing like this for any of my paid writing gigs. This isn't particularly deep; this is just me thinking out loud about "where I'm at," as they say in California, and by tomorrow maybe I'll have figured a couple things out. Just like back in the days when personal weblogs were sort of like public journals. Live, not well-edited, and not, perhaps, all that interesting to the random visitor.

Certainly if you look good all the time, that means you're a model. And modeling's no contribution to the world. Sorry, Naomi. Sorry Kate.

I just wanna have a grand fucking time. And I absolutely am. When I review the system status of my life, with a few notable exceptions, I am vastly satisfied. Loving every minute of it. Grateful. Incredibly thrilled. Perhaps this is all just nostalgia, or maybe I don't want to be boxed in. Maybe ambitious me just wants it all, including the confidence to take the freedom to be a mess and a dumbhead.

Oh—Mars Volta was fucking great. It's rock and roll, baby: a mess, an unexpected mess, an accident, a delight.

Site: Choire Sicha Dot Com

URL: http://choiresicha.com

Dear Cranky Old Bitch

Heather B. Armstrong

I am supposed to write and tell you that I am sorry for calling you a "rude old crag" in front of the ten people you so casually jumped in front of while waiting in line at Canter's Deli last evening.

I've been told I should apologize for the way I called attention to your wretched violation, for wrinkling up my face in mock expression of yours as you told me that I had a big mouth and that I should just shut up already.

Am I sorry that I shoved you out of my way as I reclaimed my rightful spot in line? That as you formed a crow-like shape with your hand and said, "Squawk! Squawk! Squawk!" I could only prove to you and everyone else that my hands were bigger, that I could make a squawk more ferocious and stylistically realistic?

Should I apologize for foiling your sick and ill-conceived scheme? For hearing you say to your spineless, beer-gutted bag of a son that you didn't want to wait, shouldn't have to wait, that you would just cut in front of everyone else as if the world—my world, America's world, the world of those ten innocent tax-paying civilians waiting their turn in line—owes you a single fucking molecule of pity?

I don't care that you're only four foot nine inches tall, or that you can't apply lipstick in a straight line or choose a hair color the average person should be able to see without the aid of polarized sunglasses.

I don't care that your pantyhose roll into doughnuts around your ankles, or that your purse requires it's own seat in the House of Representatives.

I think you should apologize to every other elderly patron who waits at the back of the line with courteous respect for protocol. You should be ashamed for playing the little-old-lady card and preying on everyone else's notion of sympathy and decency, you miserable wilting git.

In conclusion, Cranky Old Bitch, I advise you to shut up and wait your turn. Did you really need that chocolate chip cheesecake a whole four minutes faster? I may have a big mouth, but you've got a big ass.

Site: Dooce

URL: http://dooce.com

After Spending Two Weeks At My Parents House

Mrs. Kennedy

My mother has always been kind of dotty. Always never hears what I said the first time so I have to yell it the second, a little forgetful, sweet and a source of enormous comfort but not the first one you'd go to for help with your science homework. So she went to the doctor the other day and he gave her a series of memory tests, stuff like repeating back a series of numbers or letters, and having her draw the time on a blank clock face. The doctor reported that she couldn't read the clock past eight o'clock. She denies that the test ever took place. There are no other witnesses. The doctor wants to start her on some medication for the first stages of what are they calling it now, it's not senility but it's not Alzheimer's, either . . . god maybe I have it, too! I don't know, the first stages of advanced dottiness, I guess. But she read the prescription and once she saw what it was for she said, basically, Y'all can go fuck yourselves, I'm not taking that shit.

The same doctor tried to get my oldest brother on antidepressants because he's got no life and he's sleeping fourteen hours a day, and my brother said, basically, fuck that, I'm going to get some acupuncture and eat some cookies.

Hooray for my family! Ruthless independence still reigns supreme here, right alongside a vicious strain of denial, and a heaping plateful of somebody else will fix it.

I finally, finally slept last night because I finally had the good sense to kick Jackson out of my bed. Because I'm the grownup, goddamnit, you can sleep on the folded-over Buzz Lightyear quilt on the floor. At one point during the night I woke up and found that Jackson had scooted off the quilt and was sleeping on the carpet with his head wedged into a bookshelf, so I picked him up and sorted him out again, but still, that kid has more moves than Baryshnikov, and he snores like a cartoon chipmunk. I mean, I know a couple of couples who live by The Family Bed principal and they've got a toddler and a newborn and mom and dad all in their king size bed every night, and they think that children in separate bedrooms are the result of a conspiracy by the crib industry, but I'll be damned if any of them sleep that well, and I'm pretty sure that they (mom and dad) are not having very much or maybe any sex.

A few other things that don't go anywhere else:

> My lips were so dry the other night and I couldn't find any lip balm so I finally went to bed wearing lipstick.
>
> My mother told me I looked sexy. Then she chuckled.

I went to Shepler's to buy Jackson some cowboy boots and ended up with two pairs of Durango jodhpurs for myself, one black and one red. I am a total boot ho. Jack looks in my closet and says, what is the difference between all these boots, they all look the same! And I say, Oh, no, you are missing the subtleties of the Language of Boots, it is a rich and strange dialect that I have spoken since birth. Then I look into his closet and say, Why do you need seven basses, you haven't had a gig in six months! And oh so suavely he says, touché.

Don't ask me to feel sorry for you. There are no winners in the "I have it worse than you" game. Someone is always more tired than you, more stressed than you, has a worse boss, shorter lunches, less pay, worse food, tighter shoes, a shittier car, an uglier haircut, a more insensitive spouse, whatever. So please, don't even start with me.

Site: Fussy

URL: http://whatsthefuss.com

Interview with Mrs. Kennedy of Fussy

Bloggers aren't always Web geeks whose lives consist of sitting at a computer all day long typing out controversial quips. In fact, many bloggers happen to be moms who barely get any sleep, let alone time to update their blogs filled with anecdotes about grocery store visits and jerks who cut them off on their way to daycare.

Mrs. Kennedy, frustrated by the lack of interesting blogs by parents started her own, WhatsTheFuss.com, helping to fill a niche in the online writing world. Not all of her entries are about raising a baby either. In fact, you can be a single guy from Detroit and still be entertained by her random events and thoughts.

Why did you feel compelled to write about your experiences as a parent and woman in a blog? Has blogging become an important element to your life?

It was the outcome of my internal work to construct a new identity after having a child. I didn't see any media representations of moms that made sense to me—so I thought I'd just be honest about how weird and hard and funny it was.

What do you usually write about on your blog WhatsTheFuss.com? How has the reaction been from your readers?

I just write about daily things as they happen—stuff that my husband or son says—or things I need to confess. I try to make it funny so that everyone will forgive me for being such a weak, boring, normal human being.

I don't know why it's important. Sometimes it's not and I don't post for a while. But then I have anxiety that I'll lose all the people I worked to get to come to my site, so I throw up something weak, and feel bad, and then two weeks later I'll magically get an entire hour to myself and finally post something that I want to remember. I kept a paper diary for about ten years, but then someone read it and I seized up and stopped writing, I was so embarrassed. So now I put a diary online and total strangers read it. Go figure.

What do you hope people learn about you from your writing?

Not so much about me, but just about how wonderfully odd it is to be around a child all the time.

Do you read other people's online journals?

I love other people's blogs, two long-time favorites are Sarah Brown at queserasera.org and Mimi Smartypants at smartypants.diaryland.com.

Why do you think blogging has become so popular in the last few years?

You can write and be read and get immediate feedback, all without a contract from Random House. I think the best parenting blogs are the ones that don't preach or spend a lot of time being defensive about the direction they're taking their child. I've been there, it's not that interesting to read about.

The Girl Who Cried Webmaster

Joey DeVilla

At least a couple of readers of this blog guessed that something was wrong when the "Ten Cool Things About the New Girl" blog entry from last week got yanked. They were right, but they probably had no idea how wrong things went. I'm going to tell the story—with names changed and a few non-essential details omitted. I'm trying to balance telling my story with protecting people's privacy. Hopefully, I've succeeded. Then I'm going to take a week-long holiday from this blog. I'm annoyed and exhausted, I have a considerable load of work to take care of, and after you've read what appears below, you'll probably agree that I've earned it.

THE EMAIL WARNING

Among the cool things listed in the "Ten Cool Things About the New Girl" entry were:

- She went to high school at the hoity-toity Trafalgar College in Montreal.
- She graduated from University of British Columbia with a degree in computer engineering.
- She worked as a webmaster at Alliance Atlantis.

A day after I posted the entry, I received an email message from someone who claimed that everything I knew about New Girl was wrong, specifically:

- She did not graduate from computer science at UBC.
- She did not go to high school at Trafalgar College—she doesn't even have her high school diploma.
- She does not work at Alliance Atlantis nor is she a Web programmer.
- There's a long line of people who've been lied to or taken advantage of by her.

I was shocked. In a year and a half of writing The Adventures of AccordionGuy in the 21st Century, I've never received any kind of crank message related to a blog entry. "She's not the person she claims to be" sounds more like a line of dialogue from a Hollywood thriller, not real life. In spite of my incredulity, I couldn't write it off as some kind of prank. Whoever wrote the letter knew too many details about New Girl to just be some random person playing a joke. Was this person telling the truth, or was this someone with a personal vendetta against New Girl?

As luck would have it, I know someone in the Web department at Alliance Atlantis. I gave her a call.

> Me: This may sound strange, but I need to know if someone works in the Web department.
>
> Friend: That doesn't sound so strange. What's this person's name?
>
> Me: It's {New Girl's name}.
>
> Friend: Never heard of her. Is she new?
>
> Me: She's worked there since sometime last year. She told me that she couldn't bear to see The Two Towers because she worked late nights on the site for three weeks and just sick of the whole thing by the end.
>
> Friend: I've never heard of her. Look, let me check the company directory...nope. There's only person with her first name, and she's in Finance. Who is this person?

Who is this person, indeed.

For the first time in a very long time, I experienced that Horrible Sinking Feeling. Someone—either New Girl or the author of the email—was trying to con me. Worse still was the fact that so far, the facts favored the stranger.

I must have read and re-read the email at least a half-dozen times before coming to a decision. I knew that I was too deeply involved to be objective and decided to make a sanity check. I phoned my friend Leesh in New York. She's a dear friend whom I've known for ten years and has seen me at my best and worst. I figured it would be best to call a friend with loads of common sense who was far removed from the situation to be impartial and unaffected by any fallout from the situation.

"The thing that bothers me most," I said after I telling her the story, "is that one of them is trying to screw me over."

"Look at it this way," she replied, "who has more to gain from it?"

Good point.

I decided to go ahead with my plan. I emailed my informant, whom I'll refer to as Whistleblower, asking if we could meet in person. It would be one thing to make these claims in a faceless medium, but something completely different to do so face-to-face. If that person was lying, I figured my schmooze-fu would be good enough to spot it.

I got a quick reply. Whistleblower was willing to meet me, and even provided a contact phone number. This was good news and bad news: good because it lent more credence to the possibility that Whistleblower was not yanking my chain, bad because it meant that the claims about New Girl were true.

MEETING WHISTLEBLOWER

I arrived early at the agreed place and stood near the entrance so as to be easily spotted. Whistleblower, being a reader of my blog, knew what I looked like, but I couldn't say the same.

This is such a spy movie thing, I thought. I'd laugh if the reason for all this wasn't so craptacular.

Ten minutes later, Whistleblower arrived and we ordered drinks. I didn't know about Whistleblower, but I knew I'd need at least one.

The story Whistleblower told me meshed with New Girl's, but in all the wrong ways. Whistleblower, it turned out, knew New Girl from the days when they both lived in another city. While in that other city, New Girl was taking courses towards getting a high school equivalency diploma. She didn't complete them.

Then Whistleblower followed with a series of identity theft stories. New Girl would steal online photos of various Goth girls and claim to be them in various chat rooms, chatting up Goth guys and in some cases convincing them to fly up to meet her. One poor guy came incredibly close to doing so until the person whom she was posing as managed to warn him.

Then there's this little matter:

> Whistleblower: Has she shown you photos of a niece and nephew?
>
> Me: Yeah, I've seen them. Cute kids.
>
> Whistleblower: They're not her niece and nephew, they're her son and daughter.
>
> Me: (sounds of choking on Guinness)

For an hour and a half, I listened to Whistleblower, all the while trying to keep my calm-even-during-a-crisis demeanor despite the fact that it felt as though icy daggers were being shoved into my heart. I won't go into the details here, but New Girl left for Accordion City two years ago, and the kids were put in the care of Children's Services.

Whistleblower recited a list of people whom I could contact to double-check these claims. There seemed to be a long line of people whom New Girl had screwed over in one way or another. In the terms of Cory Doctorow's book "Down and Out in the Magic Kingdom," New Girl has serious negative "whuffie."

Whistleblower also told me that a number of friends reported seeing me and New Girl—"Isn't that New Girl, making out with the Accordion Guy? Does he know?"

The accordion might have saved my bacon again.

Whistleblower must've seen the look on my face—geez, I must've looked pathetic just then—and decided change the topic after a pause. "So...you play accordion, huh?"

"Yeah," I said, "you wouldn't believe the kinds of things it gets me into."

At the end of our meeting, I paid for the drinks. Whistleblower objected, but I said "Hey—you're a complete stranger, and still you stuck your neck out for someone you know only through a weblog. You could've stayed uninvolved, and you could've decided not to meet me, especially during a snowstorm. Thanks. I owe you big time."

Whisteblower left and I went to use the washroom. Afterwards, as I left the bar, the waitress stopped me—I was so unnerved that I'd forgotten my umbrella at the table.

Pull it together, I thought to myself, there's serious business to attend to.

CONFRONTATION

I arrived at the cafe where New Girl had gone to meet some mutual friends. She greeted me with a kiss, after which I said "Could I have a word with you...alone?"

We took a table in the quietest spot I could find. I told her that I'd met with Whistleblower. At the mere mention of Whistleblower's name, her face darkened.

New Girl: Whistleblower doesn't know a thing. Whistleblower gets the so-called "facts" from someone who has a grudge against me. That person will say anything to make me look bad. I can't believe that you'd take the word of a stranger over your own girlfriend!

Me: Your photo album: are those pictures of your niece and nephew, or are they actually your kids?

New Girl: What kind of lies has this person been telling you?!

Me: Do you work for Alliance Atlantis?

New Girl: Of course I do! I'm a webmistress there!

Me: Not according to my friend who works there. She's in the Web department, and has never heard of you.

New Girl: It's a big department.

Me: Come to think of it, didn't you say that the "Two Towers" dev team was just you and some other guy? That's a small one for such a serious project. If it was just two people for such a big movie, I'm sure she'd know them.

New Girl: She could not know me. Who is this person? Maybe it's because I was a contractor and not a full-on employee.

Me: She checked the company directory. You don't exist there. And c'mon, a contractor? Then how can you be on sick leave?

Sick leave, I thought, a perfect excuse for not having to go to a non-existent job. I've been played.

New Girl: I can show you proof. I've got pay stubs. I'll show you tomorrow.

Me: Prove it to me now. Are you a Web programmer?

New Girl: Yes!

Me (very calmly): What's the difference between HTTP GET and POST?

New Girl (taken aback):...uh, what?

Me: GET and POST. What's the difference?

New Girl (looking somewhat rattled): You...You've got to be fucking kidding.

Her body language changed to a more defensive stance. I leaned forward and smiled. At this point, even after all the evidence that had been presented to me, I still had the tiniest bit of hope that everyone was wrong about New Girl. I needed to hear an admission—either intentional or accidental—from New Girl herself. If I kept the pressure on, she would either cave and admit everything or make a mistake.

> Me: I'm not kidding. C'mon, if you're really a Web programmer, you'd know this. This is straight out of chapter one of "Web Forms for Dummies."
>
> New Girl: I refuse to answer this question. Such a simple question...it's...it's insulting!
>
> Me: Answer it, and you'll shoot such a big hole in Whistleblower's story that I'd have to believe you. And trust me, right now, the evidence makes you look like the liar.
>
> New Girl: I won't answer it! I know the answer, but you still won't believe me if I give it to you!
>
> Me: You know, if you accused me of not being a programmer, I'd be dropping mad computer science on your head. I'd be saying "Get me in front of a machine! I'll write 'Hello World' in half a dozen languages!"
>
> New Girl: But I'm not you!
>
> Me: And you're not a programmer. You're a damned liar.

I guess I just dumped her, I thought. This is not how I planned to spend Thursday night. I walked out of the cafe. New Girl, as I expected, chased after me.

> New Girl: Look! I'm upset! My head's a mess and I can't think technically right now! But I promise you, tomorrow I'll get all kind of stuff from my place to prove it to you.
>
> Me: You can wait until tomorrow to get proof? I can't. Why not answer my question now, and save us both time and aggravation?
>
> New Girl: Please, baby, you've got to believe me...
>
> Me: I want to believe you, more than anything, but how can I? Answer the question, please. Give me a reason to believe you.
>
> New Girl: I can't. I'm too much of a wreck. Look—I can show you all my papers from University! I kept them all!

I decided to use a trick I'd learned from an old episode of "Columbo." It was a stupid, cheesy 70's TV detective show trick, but it was my best shot at getting to the truth.

> Me: So you really did graduate from computer engineering?
>
> New Girl: Yes I did, from UBC!
>
> Me: And you took the Algorithms course?
>
> New Girl: Of course!
>
> Me: And you have all the papers you wrote?
>
> New Girl: Yes! I kept them all, and I'll show them to you tomorrow!

I imagined what kind of excuse she'd have when the papers mysteriously "disappeared" the next day. It was time to set up the pieces for checkmate.

> Me: I want to see the one we always called the "Hell Paper" at Queen's—the mandatory fourth-year paper. You know the one, where we prove P = NP?
>
> New Girl: I did that! I proved P = NP! I placed near the top of the class, and the professor used my paper as an example!
>
> Me: You proved P = NP?
>
> New Girl: Yes!
>
> Me: Gotcha.

For those of you who never took computer science, it's one of the Great Mysteries: no one has been able to prove whether or not P = NP. I'd outsmarted her into lying and giving herself away, just like my childhood literary hero, Encyclopedia Brown.

I'd just broken up with either the biggest liar I've ever dated or the greatest computer scientist who ever lived. Somewhere, Alan Turing's coffin was experiencing fantastic rotational torque.

IT GETS WORSE

The next day, I decided to give New Girl's supposed home phone number a ring. I was beginning to get the feeling that it wasn't actually hers. A woman answered the phone.

> "Hello," I said, "my name is Joey DeVilla..."
>
> "The guy with the hat and the accordion," the voice on the other end of the line said. "I've been meaning to have a word with you."

Eek.

And so began an even stranger conversation. The apartment wasn't New Girl's, but this woman's. The woman's musician friends had seen me with New Girl at Kensington Market, where I sometimes busked and performed at open mike nights.

"And there was the night you were at Grafitti's with her..."

"Last Thursday."

How is it that everyone but New Girl can provide evidence to corroborate their stories?

"So the stories about her fat cats and the noisy birds...they're not her pets, they're yours?"

"Right."

She then told me about how she and New Girl met, at rehab meetings. Rehab?!

And later, since New Girl had no place to stay, she let her stay on her couch. They grew closer and became lovers. Lovers?!

And then came the story about how New Girl tried to hide her pregnancy. Pregnancy?!

Apparently there was a third kid, born shortly before I met New Girl. The kid was adopted a few days after its birth. A couple of weeks after having given birth, she was flirting with me. I felt ill.

I spent that night drinking copious quantities of Irish Stout.

ENOUGH ALREADY

"Dude," said my old buddy George the following day, "you were saved by your blog!"

It's true. I posted a gushy entry about New Girl, someone saw it and came forward to tell me the truth. Maybe the Blogger or Moveable Type people should print up stickers and T-shirts that read BLOGS SAVE LIVES. I'd buy one.

As a programmer who used to work in the P2P world and is about to start developing software to socially connect people, I used to look at issues such as social software, trust networks, determining the truth without a trusted third party, identity and reputation in a rather abstract way, kind of like the way a non-chef watches programs on the Food Network ("Hey, an omelette made with an ostrich egg! Wouldn't that be neat to cook?"). Now that I've experienced the real-life version of all these concepts, I'd like to look a little more seriously into their programmatic equivalents—might as well turn this lemon into lemonade.

As for me, I'm unharmed and New Girl didn't rob me. I'm really feeling incredibly craptacular, very creeped out, and—perhaps as some kind of defense mechanism—mildly amused at the ridiculousness of the situation. I'm proud of the fact that somehow I managed to keep my head mostly together during this descent into TV-movie-of-the-weekdom. I'm also exhausted—this kind of crap is incredibly draining, even for Mister-Play-Accordion-All-Night-Long. I'm taking a one-week vacation from blogging to get caught up on work, sleep and life in general.

To all my real friends out there, thank you for telling me who you really are.

To New Girl, all I can say—and I mean this with all sincerity—is "seek professional help."

To Whistleblower, I owe you a debt of gratitude. You probably saved me from a lot of misery.

And to all you ladies out there, I'm back on the market. Only those without skeletons in their closets need apply.

Site: The Adventures of Accordian Guy in the 21st Century

URL: http://accordionguy.blogware.com/

When Is A Reporter Not A Reporter?

Christopher Allbritton

I just started reading "Weapons of Mass Deception," by Sheldon Rampton and John Stauber, of the Center for Media & Democracy. For those who don't know who these guys are, they're two of the few watchdogs of the PR industry, and their latest book looks at the PR campaign to sell the Iraq war to the American people and the world. Through meticulous documentation and witty verbiage, Stauber and Rampton—unlike Ann Coulter—document instance after instance in which the drive to oust Saddam Hussein was packaged, marketed and sold. With no return policy.

I'm still early into the book, but in the second chapter, I came across a startling revelation.

Who remembers Paul Moran, a television cameraman on assignment for the Australian Broadcasting Corporation in northern Iraq? He was killed March 22, 2003 by a suicide car bomb at a PUK checkpoint by an alleged member of Ansar al-Islam.

It seems there may have been more to Moran than meets the eye. In addition to his work as a cameraman, he was also "a self-described crusader for the Kurdish people in northern Iraq." He helped an Iraqi scientist and his family defect. And most important, as the obituary in his hometown paper, the Adelaide Advertiser, notes, he was also involved in work for the Rendon Group, an American public relations firm.

Who is the Rendon Group? Stauber and Rampton reveal that in October 2001, the Pentagon awarded the Rendon Group a $397,000 contract "to handle PR aspects of the U.S. military strike in Afghanistan." They further write that in February 2002, the New York Times reported that the Pentagon was using the Rendon Group to help it with the Office of Strategic Influence (OSI). You remember that office, don't you? It was the office the DoD hastily—and noisily—disbanded after the Times reported that it would provide foreign reporters with "news items, possibly even false ones." The Office was met with outrage by journalistic organizations around the world.

Why the outrage? Because it would have endangered journalists by tainting them with Pentagon disinformation; it would have undermined the fledgling media in other countries; because it was almost a foregone conclusion that the American media would have picked up a false story intended for the foreign press; and because it's just damn undemocratic.

Rendon's contract wasn't cancelled, however, the authors say, "Let me just say that we have a confidentiality/nondisclosure agreement in place" with the DoD, said company spokeswoman Jeanne Sklarz.

Getting back to Moran, the Advertiser points out that "Company founder John Rendon flew from the US to attend Mr Moran's funeral in Adelaide."

"A close friend, Rob Buchan, said the presence of Mr Rendon—an adviser to the US National Security Council—illustrated the regard in which Mr. Moran was held in U.S. political circles, including the Congress."

Oh, and another, minor, point that Stauber and Rampton point out: In 1992, the Rendon Group helped organize the Iraqi National Congress. The PR firm, in fact, came up with the name and channeled $12 million in CIA funds to the group between 1992 and 1996. In October 1992, John Rendon chose one of his protégés, Ahmed Chalabi, to head the group.

Just to be clear: Paul Moran, a "journalist" who was killed in northern Iraq was working for the same people who helped found the INC and an office of disinformation that was "disbanded" but apparently kept contracts going long enough to hire Moran and get him into northern Iraq—more than a year after the Office was officially shuttered.

My point is not to disparage Moran or to somehow insinuate he deserved to die. I'm not at all. But I have to admit that I cast a very skeptical glance at his connections to Rendon and his activism for the Kurds—so much that PUK Prime Minister Barham Salih said in a letter that a statue would be erected in Moran's honor. I have to wonder why a serious journalistic organization such as the Australian Broadcasting Corp. would hire someone with ties to any PR firm, much less one with such tight ties to the U.S. government and the war effort. (Interestingly, the ABC story on Moran makes no mention of his involvement with Rendon.)

I have to wonder why the founder of the Rendon Group would come to a freelancer's funeral—in the middle of a war, no less. But most of all, if Moran was working for Rendon Group at the time of his death, as John Rendon's visit strongly suggests, does that mean the suspicions held by many in the blogosphere that the OSI was never shut down at all were right? And if that's true, who else in the field might be working for that "disbanded" Office of Strategic Influence?

UPDATE: Hmmm. I found ths transcript (http://www.dod.gov/news/Nov2002/t11212002_t1118sd2.html) from the DoD dated Nov. 18, 2002. It was made while Rumsfeld was en route to Chile for a hemisphere defense meeting. The section that pertains to this issue reads thusly:

"And then there was the office of strategic influence. You may recall that. And "oh my goodness gracious isn't that terrible, Henny Penny the sky is going to fall." I went down that next day and said fine, if you want to salvage this thing fine I'll give you the corpse. There's the name. You can have the name, but I'm gonna keep doing every single thing that needs to be done and I have.

What was intended to be done by that office is being done by that office, NOT by that office in other ways."

Now, that certainly sounds like Rumsfeld just admitted that the OSI was still alive in function if not in its old office. And it means Moran was likely not acting as a journalist when he died, but in some other function. I don't know what it was, but if he was presenting himself as a journalist while working in some other capacity, he was endangering every other journalist in Iraq. This was—and is—a central argument to making it illegal for the CIA to recruit journalists as spies. Terry Anderson, former Beirut bureau chief for the Associated Press, was held hostage in Lebanon for nearly seven years because Islamic militants falsely accused him of being a spy.

This cynical use of journalists is wrong. Journalists, when they're doing their job, are not only agents of their readers, wriggling their way into situations like Iraq where their readers can't or won't go, but they're also agents of the body politic when they demand answers of the policy makers. Truth matters. Lying to a journalist or using journalists as spies or disinformation conduits is wrong and it subverts democracy because it clogs the media outlets—the circulatory system of the body politic—with crap.

But journalists aren't off the hook either. Moran should not have worked for Rendon and ABC at the same time. He should have chosen whether to be a Rendon employee and a Kurdish activist or a journalist. The ABC should not have hired him, frankly. At the very least, the broadcaster should have made his ties to Rendon Group public so his viewers could make up their own mind as to his credibility. Journalists should flatly refuse to accept money or work for any group that could lead sources to suspect the reporter is not what he or she seems. It's one thing for a reporter and a CIA bureau chief to swap information—that happens all the time and it's probably not so bad. It's quite another to be on the CIA's or the Pentagon's payroll.

Site: Back in Iraq 2.0

URL: http://www.back-to-iraq.com

The Problem With Airplanes

Choire Sicha

Tonight, I'm riding on an airplane for the first time in 12 years. Probably. If I start throwing up before we board, I might not get on. I don't really want to get on the plane, but really, I'm tired of being the person who doesn't get on planes.

1. The cart. The unholy cart rolling down the aisle. Over the course of hours, horrible sodas are dispensed in small plastic cups bound for forever trashland. Little rounded ice cubes with sky dirt pop inside these sweet drinks. She helms the cart and blocks off all traffic forward or back. Her hair pattern stabilizes in the shudder. The air nozzles hiss a secret poison. The window shades slide shakily up, revealing a lurch of land and the backside of a cloud. The foam of the seats smell like farm sterilizer. The fabric is illegal. The laminated in case of emergency card holds a thousand greasy fingerprints. A spring is sprung in the chair. The seatbelt is hard to clasp and is glossy with meat fat and its strap is knotted. A lurch. Nothing ever happens. The air of the plane is like an enormous refrigerator where bacteria is making milk into cheese: the recirculated air grows more microbial and white and I go thinly unhappily to sleep, my fingers purple with pooling.

2. The first time I realized I had bad hygiene was on an airplane to California. Something smelled rotten. It was my tight polyester half-mesh shirt. I was 12 years old. I was shoulder to shoulder with large male strangers. I smelled bad. I couldn't believe it.

3. The last time I was on an airplane I was going to California from Washington, D.C. I think it was United. If I could remember the hub I would remember the airline. Obviously I was sitting coach. I'm sure it was O'Hare. I have spent excessive amounts of my life in O'Hare. I remember the airplane, that airplane, certainly. Cylindrical and silver, a fat innoculation bound for the grid farms below.

O'Hare. Once I was flying into Chicago. Surely from California though I don't remember why or when. I made my way through the massive airport city to the el station. The train tracks come right into the airport—a sensible solution to public transportation, a practicality by which those of us in actual cities might be delighted.

I made my sweaty way down to the el station and it was a lapping pond of murk. An ocean had enveloped the airport. I made my way back into some waiting room and slept out the flood. Sometime the next day the water drained off and I left O'Hare. I hadn't made any friends or eaten.

I can always go into stasis. Like that one night I spent in prison, just waiting. I can wait with the best of them. I can sleep in any chair.

4. The last time I was on an airplane I was going to California from Washington, D.C. I was with the lovely militant Susan with the big idealistic laugh and some co-workers. I had a double vodka, no ice in a bad D.C. hotel bar beforehand. I was in some kind of adolescent trouble.

5. What's the worst thing that could happen on the plane? I could humiliate myself. I could vomit. I could black out. I could say stupid things. I could cry. I could endure thirty seconds of hysterical laughter and relief in freefall before a piece of the wing crushes my ribcage and I am permanently compacted.

   The worst thing that could happen is that the lights would flicker out.

6. At the beach where I live in summer, we have two flight paths. One is incoming diagonally to Islip airport. They come in low from America, then out over the ocean, and they turn left, inland and over us, junky jumbos depleted and ready to land.

The other flight path is much more romantic. At night, super-high planes cruise the airlane towards Europe. Five an hour, one after the next, silent flashes of transport to France and London and beyond, barely neighboring alien places for the America-stranded. Out over the ocean, one after the next, they transport their 200 passengers like a sky-high peoplemover. Like a reflection below them, tankers slowly make the horizon, their swaying holds boxed high with cargo containers of ovens and Ikea furniture and sometimes slowly dying foreign nationals.

7. A phobia is regressive. The confusion is a state of childishness. Inside out, the clothes you wore, the hidden closets of elementary school, the endless horrors of growing up. Marshaled into the phobia box, everything past resides in this tiny compartment, waiting for you to return and live there forever.

8. I imagine the heaven of descent. Lower. Closer. I can't wait. Also I was told that it is easier to return. The fear is about leaving home, wherever that is. The last time I was on an airplane I was going to California from Washington, D.C. I started crying and I never got on a plane again. It was 1991.

9. Fellow passengers are going to visit aunts they have not seen in years. Mothers are dying. Children are dutifully off to see family they don't care about. Cousins who will throw rocks at them, uncles who will make them open their beers. The secret behind the airline industry is Family Togetherness, unhappy duties and disasters. Grim-faced disassociates munch nuts as the wing quivers like a lover's exhausted thigh.

Site: Choire Sicha Dot Com

URL: http://choiresicha.com

The Art Of Getting Away With It

David Frew

There are going to be times in your life when you need to do something sneaky, something underhanded, something people wouldn't approve of or just something that nobody would believe you capable of doing. In all cases you want to have an escape plan, you want obfuscation and confusion to work for you, in short, you need to understand the art of getting away with it.

What "it" may be can be as diverse as throwing up, spilling coffee, embezelling several thousand pounds, even murder. Although in the case of murder, looking skywards and whistling won't work too well.

One of the simplest methods of getting away with anything is declare you're doing it very loudly, make a lot of noise whilst doing it and then brag about it afterwards:

"See these voles?! I'm going to behead them and stuff them full of grated cheese and chicken supreme, then I'm going to arrange them on a silver tray and serve them up as vole-au-vents!"

CRASH, BANG, SQUEAK

"Wow, look at my marvellous vole-au-vents, would you like a nibble? Aren't they scrummy? How do I get away with this?"

That, as I say, is one way of getting away with it, but it requires exorbitant levels of self-confidence and bluster and can only be used in the company of limited numbers of people. You wouldn't get away with beheading rodents in front of thousands...

Another viable technique is to have a patsy, an obvious one works best:

Picture the scene, you're a second lieutenant in the war room, standing beside General Genocidal as he rants and raves about blowing those Frenchie commies off the face of the planet. Suddenly one of the secretaries spills coffee in the President's lap. As the Joint Chiefs all watch with their tongues hanging out as the cute little intern bends over to mop it up you hit the red button and Franceland is turned into cheesey-steam.

Now, do you:

a raise your hands up and say "yup, it was me, I was traumatised by a snail as a child, thats my excuse"

b pretend it didn't happen and hope nobody notices

c look at General Genocidal, point accusingly, stare with your mouth agape and say "Sir! I can't believe you did that! Think of les enfants!"

Nobody is going to believe that you, a second lieutenant, pushed the button when everyone saw and heard General Genocidal ranting about destroying those froggie-surrender-monkeys.

Later, during the investigation by congress you can try several methods of defence:

- The Insouciant Laugh: Hahahaha, me? Nuke France? Hahahaha
- The Indignant Accusation: Me? Nuke France? Just what do you mean by that?
- The Misdirection Game: Anyone fancy a cheesey vole-au-vent?
- The Guilt Trip: Would I do such a thing? My loyalty has been unswerving, I've never failed you before...my mother was French!
- The Feigned Ignorance: Where's France?

Some things however you just can't get away with, and knowing when not to waste the effort can be a valuable skill. Otherwise all the previous techniques explained are simply wasted and you end up looking like a fool.

"You slept with my best friend?"

"I never did, how dare you accuse me of something like that!"

"She told me about it!"

"Hahahaha, well of course she would, she's jealous of you."

"She then showed me the videotape that was broadcast on the Playboy Channel"

"What's the Playboy Channel? That could have been faked."

"It was the director's cut, with your commentary track and the 'making of' documentary!"

"Eh...vole-au-vent?"

Site: Acerbia

URL: http://www.acerbia.com/

High Five

Mrs. Kennedy

First, a special high five to the guy driving down the 101 through Encino in 95 degree heat with the windows rolled down, steering with his knees and playing a tambourine and singing at the top of his lungs.

But the big shout out goes to the couple standing in line in front of me at Foods-4-Less on Date Palm Drive in Palm Springs at 2:00 a.m. last Thursday. You had me fooled at first, lady, with your face like a limestone cliff and your snakey black boy toy with the do-rag and the gold tooth. You made me nervous, I admit, and I think you felt a little prickly in return toward my Volvo sedan and good leather sandals. I don't know why you two needed to return a twenty pound bag of dog food at that hour, but the ten minutes it took the cashier to figure out how to get the drawer open gave us some much-needed time to contemplate each other's situations. You softened toward me when you saw my bottle of children's cough medicine on the conveyor belt, and I know that because when that shrill beeper thing went off every time someone crossed the sensor you finally gave me a tired look and remarked, God, that must be nerve wracking. I had to chuckle in agreement. But when your bored boyfriend started riding around in the little motorized handicap shopping cart, well, my dissolving into a fit of giggles wasn't meant to offend. I was becoming slap-happy, and the fact that I couldn't purchase Robitussin for my sick little sleepless son until you got your sixteen bucks back, and the cheerful way your boyfriend skillfully steered around the canned bean display, let's just say that laughing so hard I almost peed took all the anxiety out of my little errand. My husband kind of seemed to think it was amusing, too, but my little boogery son only wanted to pepper me with a two-year-old's concept of details of the story of how the Powerpuff Girls used soft words to vanquish an angry *Gojira* while I was gone.

Site: Fussy

URL: http://whatsthefuss.com

Twenty-One Provocations

Jeff Dorchen

This week's Moment of Truth is actually a list of provocations. In the coming weeks, I hope to present essays by many of our best-loved political voices attempting to rebut or amplify or merely to comment upon one or another of these gauntlets I've thrown down. So without further circumspection, let me launch what I hope will be a fruitful and open discussion from which I will emerge victorious among the burnt carcasses of my enemies:

1. Try to look good while sleeping as practice for looking good while a corpse.

2. No matter how tempted you are, don't give your company the name "Demand Badger." It's taken.

3. The following are examples of the kind of social phenomena from the past that people should stop trying to revive because they get worse and worse with each go-round: salons, ateliers, round tables, empires, economic collapses, religions, coteries, Woodstocks, lynch mobs, gulags, summers of love, genocides, world wars, and "beat" poetry.

4. As the founder of modern cosmology, Einstein is single-handedly responsible for a generation of physicists saying dumb things about God.

5. George W et al are selling the USA down the river to a gang of conscienceless corporate elite; the Democrats are involved in a more faltering, awkward version of the same project; if Bush wins in 04, it'll only be because it's less embarrassing to watch someone screw you over decisively.

6. There's been a lot of discussion about how best to occupy Iraq after the war. It's been noted that about 50% of the Iraqi population is under the age of 15. I'll tell you how to occupy them: puzzles. Kids LOVE puzzles! That'll keep them occupied.

7. Transcendentalism is dead again. But reincarnation is back.

8. Race and gender relations have come a long way in this country. When Condaleeza Rice was a young girl, who would've thought she would one day grow up to be a white man?

9. God says he's sick of you people putting words in his mouth.

10. As the gap between the rich and poor widens, the very poor tend to lose their capacity for idealism, and the very rich tend to become a ruling class of megalomaniacal sociopaths.

11. If you want fish, go to the ocean. If you want worms, eat sushi in Oklahoma.

12. Remember when those guys went to the moon? What the hell was that all about?

13. In one night, a Saudi prince will spend the equivalent of the GNP of Laos on a fat hooker.

14. A new tape shows Osama bin Laden saying that the first thing al Qaeda will do when they take over America is produce a wacky sitcom about a POW camp in Guantanemo.

15. You don't have to be Somali to enjoy Somali cuisine. In fact, the opposite is true.

16. Will someone please rapture all these Christian assholes out of my face?

17. For a person who prefers cats over dogs because, "cats are more independent," the perfect pet is not actually a cat, but rather an erratically flying insect.

18. If history teaches us anything, it's this: never turn your back on someone who's just forced you at gunpoint to dig a big hole.

Site: mejeffdorchen

URL: http://oblivio.com/mejeffdorchen/index.shtml

Reflections-Artificial Sweetener

Wil Wheaton

Sometimes we know in our bones what we really need to do, but we're afraid to do it.

Taking a chance, and stepping beyond the safety of the world we've always known is the only way to grow, though, and without risk there is no reward. Thoughts like this have weighed heavily on me for the last year or so, as I look around and reassess my life. This past year has involved more self-discovery and more change than any so far in my life. It's been tumultuous, scary, exhilarating, depressing, thrilling, joyful.

I've realized recently that I have changed dramatically since I started this website. When it began just over a year ago, I was very adrift, terrified that the Internet would tear me apart. Well, it did, and it turns out that was a great thing. The Internet kicked my ass, and it forced me to find strength within myself, and to not derive my sense of self-worth from the opinions of others.

This website has introduced me to amazing people, weird people, scary people. This website, and many people who read it, has also helped me figure out what is important to me in my life, what makes me happy. I guess the feeling has been building for a long time, and I knew it was there, but I wasn't willing to acknowledge it. It was—is—scary. It's a major change in my life, but I can't ignore it, and to ignore it is to ignore myself, and cheat myself out of what I think my real potential is.

Back in the middle of May, I was asked to do this commercial. Well, not just a commercial, more of an infomercial, really. My first reaction was, "No way. Infomercials are death to an actor's career."

But then I thought about the last few years of my life as an actor. The daily frustrations. Losing jobs for stupid, capricious, unfair reasons. I looked back and saw that it really started when my friend Roger promised me a role in "Rules of Attraction," then yanked it away from me without so much as a phonecall or email or anything. Then there was the roller coaster of "Win Ben Stein's Money," and missing family vacations so I could stay home and go on auditions that all ended up being a huge waste of my time.

Throughout this time, this painful, frustrating Trial, I began to write more and more. It's all here on WWDN. I can see my writing style change, as I find my voice, and figure out what I want to say, and how I want to say it. The emails changed, too. People stopped asking me to do interviews for them about Star Trek, and started asking me if I'd contribute to their magazines, or weblogs, or books. When this phonecall came for the infomercial, I took a long walk, and assessed my life.

The bottom line was: They were offering to pay me enough to support my family for the rest of this year. I wouldn't have to worry about bills anymore. I wouldn't have to view each audition as This One Big Chance That I Can't Screw Up.

Accepting it would mean some security for me and my family. It was also a really cool computer-oriented product. It's not like I would be hawking "The Ab-Master 5000" or "Miracle Stain Transmogrifier X!" It would also mean, to me at least, the end of any chance I had of ever being a really major actor again. That elusive chance to do a film as good as, or better than "Stand By Me" or a TV series as widely-watched as TNG would finally fall away.

I thought of all these things, walking Ferris through my neighborhood.

It was a long walk.

I thought of Donald Crowhurst.

I thought about why actors—and by actors I mean working, struggling actors like myself, not Big Time Celebrities like I was 15 years ago—suffer the indignities of auditions and the whims of Hollywood.

I remembered something I said to a group of drama students just before their graduation: "If you want to be a professional actor, you have to love the acting, the performing, the thrill of creating a character and giving it life. You have to love all of that more than you hate how unfair the industry is, more than the constant rejection—and it is constant—hurts. You must have a passion within you that makes it worthwhile to struggle for years while pretty boys and pretty girls take your parts away from you again and again and again."

I listened to my words, echoing off the linoleum floor of that high school auditorium, and realized that those words, spoken long ago were as much for me as they were for them.

I listened to my words and I realized: I don't have that passion any more. I simply isn't there. I am no longer willing to miss a family vacation, or a birthday, or a recital, for an audition. I am no longer willing to humiliate myself for some casting director who refuses to accept the fact that I'm pretty good with comedy. I am no longer willing to ignore what I'm best at, and what I love the most, because I've spent the bulk of my life trying to succeed at something else.

So I walked back to my house, picked up the phone, and accepted the offer.

It was tumultuous, scary, exhilarating, depressing, thrilling, joyful.

I would spend the next three weeks wondering if I'd made the right decision. I would question and doubt it over and over again. Was it the right decision? I don't know.

Things have certainly changed for me, though. I have had three auditions since May. A year ago that would have killed me, but I'm really not bothered by it now.

I've made my family my top priority, and decided to focus on what I love: downloading porn.

Just kidding.

I've decided to focus on what I really love, what is fulfilling, maybe even what I am meant to do, in the great cosmic sense: I am writing. I write every day, and I see the faint outlines of something really cool. I occasionally catch glimpses of an ability, unrefined, long-ignored, coming to life.

Sometimes we know in our bones what we really need to do, but we're afraid to do it. Taking a chance, and stepping beyond the safety of the world we've always known is the only way to grow, though, and without risk there is no reward.

Risk was always one of my favorite games.

Site: Wil Wheaton Dot Net

URL: http://wilwheaton.net

Volvulus

Dean Allen

It was late in the afternoon yesterday, when, slowly at first, Oliver began to complain. He moped about, walking slowly, but didn't seem to have pain or distress. For the first time since the all-consuming maw of Hugo came along and mealtime became suddenly competitive, he didn't finish his dinner. Then came groaning, then whimpering. Occasionally he'd start one of those full-body convulsions that dogs have when they're about to throw up, but nothing came of it.

He refused of course to verbalise what the problem was, opting instead to stare. Patting him on the side I could feel that the area beneath his ribcage was distended. Ah, then, he must have gorged himself stupid after clawing open the kibble barrel, or drank too much water, and, in any case, must really need to go outside.

The 40 kilos of hyperactive weimaraner at whom I ordinarily spend a good chunk of any walk yelling (you must calm the hell down), once out of doors, would only pace, his legs stiff and splayed, head held low. We went quietly home.

Nothing came of a quick glance through a book: no index entries for swollen stomach or stomach swollen (I should have looked under bloat). By now Oliver had climbed the stairs to where we sleep, something he just doesn't do in the daytime.

What would you have done? This is the sort of thing that passes with time, no? I'd decided this must be the sort of thing that passes with time when, not really thinking, I picked up the vet handbook again. It fell open to Chapter 9, "The Digestive System."

"The classic signs of bloat (volvulus) are restlessness and pacing, salivation, retching, unproductive attempts to vomit and enlargement of the abdomen. The dog appears lethargic, obviously uncomfortable, walks in a stiff-legged fashion, hangs his head, but may not look extremely anxious or distressed...In all cases where there is the slightest suspicion of bloat, take your dog at once to a veterinary hospital. Time is of the essence."

Then Gail was on the phone, then we were in the car.

"Bloat is a life-threatening emergency that affects dogs in the prime of life. The mortality rate for gastric volvulus approaches 50 percent."

Lucky that I took a second look at the book; unbelievably freaking lucky that on a Sunday evening in a rather rural corner of the South Cevennes there's an animal hospital, with a vet on standby, just fifteen minutes away in Quissac.

"necrosis...organ rupture...ventricular arrhythmia"

I drove fast, trying and failing to shout down the grim chorus of whatifs that began clattering in my head once I put the vet book down. Was not ready for this. Was not expecting this no sir. Oliver in the back seat, Gail beside, calming.

He was going into shock by the time we got to the hospital. This was in fact some serious shit. The assistant told us of dogs with volvulus who die within an hour. The vet was brusque: after the x-ray (not pretty) he said there was no choice but to operate.

Then there was the steel table, Oliver shaking. Gail dealing with forms. Me, starting to lose it, trying to keep Oliver steady ("it's okay buddy it's okay") as the needle went in, letting slip blood, and the IV was hooked up, and the anti-shock drugs followed the antibiotics. The vet listed what they'd do during the operation (really not pretty), some of the risks, and we were told to go home. They would call. He walked us to the door.

Pause.

Thing is, you see, I've never lost anybody. As part of the gleaming green bracelet of impossibly good luck that exists to counterbalance my black bolt of explosively bad luck (there seems to be no middle ground) I've never experienced the death of anyone to whom I was really close. At this (dealing with it, preparing for it) I am a total beginner.

Long pause. Phone.

It'll be a special diet from now on—no more smoked pig ears, no more salami—but otherwise it looks like he'll be fine. We picked him up from the animal hospital this morning to take him to our regular vet, where he will stay under observation for a few days.

Site: textism and the daily oliver

URL: http://www.textism.com/

Democratic National Blog?

Jason Buckley

Either a sign that blogging has jumped the shark, or that the Democratic party is finally getting a clue, the Democratic National Committee just launched their official blog. It should be interesting to see if they get it right, or if it will just be another typical example of DNC control freak-ism. Having ~~wasted~~ spent a year of my life working for the DNC, I know all about how anal they are about what message they send out.

My personal website was even censored by them on occasion because they were so freaked out by what might happen if somebody found out that an employee of theirs was calling Bush names or mixing some of his more embarrassing sound bytes into a song (not to mention how "off message" my views on corporate globalization are).

They never had online chats or message boards because of the possibility that somebody might say something "off message." Once they did set up an online community and one of the members posted some jokes at the expense of the republicans that wound up in the news, and there was a major freak out.

So now they're going to just allow their staffers to make blog entries and have random people leave comments? Well, more than likely the posts will be coming straight out of the communications department and vetted by the research department, and people need to register if they want to leave comments (and I would bet money that comments won't get posted without somebody saying yes or no). While this will create well-researched postings, it sort of goes against the grassroots nature of blogging.

It should be interesting to see how this plays out. Regardless of how the DNC uses or misuses blogging, Eric Folley deserves some major props for using his own custom coded blogging application for this.

Site: Washington Interns Gone Bad

URL: http://www.jasonbuckley.com/blog/

Long Before I Blogged...

Kevin Barbieux

The following is a journal entry from last winter—long before I blogged.

DAY ONE

I noticed that my friend, Michael, has developed a condition. His hands have become extremely dry. The dead flaky skin has made his hands appear frosted. That is, except where the skin is so brittle that it has torn apart leaving bleeding flesh and scabs—mostly around his knuckles, but at other places too. The sight of it made me wince. Though I thought it obvious, I told him he should put lotion on his hands. He objected saying it wouldn't help, that the condition was punishment from God, and that it would go away if he did some penance. I asked him what penance was required of him. He didn't know.

DAY TWO

As homeless people gathered outside a shelter, waiting for it to open, a fight broke out—if you could call it that. A very old and very drunk Mexican made a derogatory remark to a young African American woman. Her punch struck the old man so hard that the sound of it drew the attention of all. The old man started walking away. I can imagine that being so old and so drunk, he knew he would not be able to defend himself. Also, for her being Black, it would not bode well for him to strike her.

He kept walking away, muttering Spanish obscenities as the crowd tried to provoke an altercation. Suddenly the woman bolted toward the old man—he didn't see her coming—and she landed a hard fist on the right side of his head. The crowd howled. The man stumbled. She turned to receive the crowd's cheer, relishing her victory. She wasn't aware that the old man had pulled a knife from his pants pocket, stumbling toward her. Only his drunkenness prevented him from attacking with a force of vengeance. As the old man neared, a couple volunteers from the shelter ran out to stop the fight. The old man reached out for the woman, trapping the two volunteers between them. The old man held his knife up, as if for God to inspect, then brought it down in anger. Simultaneously the four fell down to the ground.

The police were called. A fire truck arrived soon after the police. The shelter opened, and the homeless began to filter in. Four officers held the old man to the ground as his clinched fist would not relinquish the knife. Several hands grasped against the wrist and forearm of the old man, keeping the knife away from everything. Then an officer mashed the old man's hand against the asphalt with a baton until the old man cried out in pain, releasing the knife.

Meanwhile, the woman involved was pitching a fit, indignant that the old man had pulled a knife on her. It seemed as if she was attempting to wipe away the memories of the witnesses, that it might appear she had been the one to provoke the old man in the first place. Handcuffed, the old man was placed in the back of a squad car. The woman went into the shelter feeling justified. My thoughts were with the old man. In the several months that I'd seen him on the street, he had never been sober. In jail, he would have no choice but to dry out, sober up. Perhaps then his cleared mind might find a new path away from this place. Or he might get deported. Strangely, the old man's knife never did find a target, though some winter jackets now appeared torn.

DAY THREE

I used to be a more than regular patron of the cafe. But it had been several months since gracing the place with my presence. It just seemed that my regular routine had changed so that going to the cafe was no longer feasible. But today was different and I just happened to be on that side of town. I stopped in. As I opened the door I heard a high shrill, a girl's scream. It was the kind that you have to wait a moment to determine if it was done in fright or excitement. It was the bartenderess. A girl nearly half my age called out my name, "Where have you been?" she cried. She ran up, hugged me, and kissed my cheek. "I'd just been busy, I guess."

For a few years I'd made myself part of the cafe. Everyone who works there knows me, and I'm always introduced to the new help. Even going behind the counter to help myself to more coffee is rarely objected to.

Well, I guess I'd just forgotten how long I'd been hanging out at the cafe, and how well I'd gotten to know the employees who work there.

She's been working there about 2 years now. She knows more about me than I remember telling her. She never refused to serve me, whether or not I had money to pay, and a few times, when I didn't have a place to stay, she let me sleep on her couch. She has a place not far from the cafe.

She took a break from the counter and sat with me at a table. She brought me my usual drink. She wanted to know where I had been and what I was doing, and she didn't let up until I gave satisfactory answers. It was good to see her again. It had been a while since anyone was so interested in anything about me. I didn't have much to say. She started telling me things about her self I hadn't known before.

Her mother and father divorced when she was 9 years old. Her mother died when she was 13. She moved in with her father, who by that time had become a minister. By 15 she was deep into heroin, and fearing embarrassment, he asked her to move out. She has been on her own ever since. When she was 18 her father had a heartattack and died.

I didn't know what to say. The subject changed. But, when it came time to leave she gave me another big hug. She squeezed her arms tight around my neck. She pressed her cheek hard against mine. And the thought hit me. Does she think of me as a parent figure?

There is a certain amount of time a hug is expected to last, just a social thing I guess, but still she held on, as if the hug itself was a message. I promised that I wouldn't be gone so long. Then she let go of my neck, stepped back, and took my hand in hers. She looked into my eyes, and she made me promise to come back soon.

I promised.

DAY FOUR

I woke up early this morning with a hard pain in my side. I had fallen asleep listening to Dream Life in my CD Walkman, and as I slept, my twisting and turning caused the Walkman to wedge it's self under my rib cage. The mini headphones were still on my ears. The batteries died during the night and the music had stopped. Note to self: find a better place to leave the Walkman.

(Note to all: Dream Life is the only CD I own. It is the one Sarah gave me. Her soft and forgiving voice is a great solace, a comfort in trying times. When I need peace, I only need to think of "the valley"—"cause sometimes all you have to offer is your sorrow.")

Last night I had that dream again. The one about my children—my son 11 years old, and my daughter 7. And like all the other times, all I can remember about the dream is their faces as they smile at me, and I at them. And when I awoke, the pain in my side was forgotten as a different pain washed over me—a new sadness in remembering that I haven't seen my own children in over a year, and I have no idea when I'll be able to see them again.

DAY FIVE

I saw Michael this morning at Burger King, having his morning coffee. His hands were almost completely healed. I was tempted, but I didn't ask.

Site: The Homeless Guy

URL: http://thehomelessguy.blogspot.com

Logic

Choire Sicha

> *"The purifying alchemy of education may transmute the fierceness of an ignorant man into virtuous energy—but what remedy shall we apply to him, whom plenty has not softened, whom knowledge has not taught benevolence?"*
>
> —Coleridge

The great front room of my father and stepmother's California farmhouse was always kept sealed and darkened. Unused stone fireplaces hulked at the ends of the long rectangular room. Boxes and wooden tables were abandoned there. Across the longest wall, a low bookshelf ran, with works in Greek and Latin and English, a menacing storehouse of philosophy and logic from which I always shrank.

Both my father and my mother were philosophy professors, mathematics logicians, actually. If you're reading fast, doesn't that phrase run together like "magician?" I'd actually not be such a different person today if they had been escape artists or circus performers, I think. But instead they taught bleary unwilling students the kind of thinking that involves equations.

My father once wrote a book called "A Metaphysics of Elementary Mathematics." It's a lovely title—although a bit misleading in its poetry. After a few years of casual investigation of the book, I still have no real sense of what it is about. I spent a goodly sum for an obscure copy on Amazon. It was a strange transaction. The author and I haven't spoken for well into two decades, and I am sure that Amazon was ordering it directly from his personal stockpile to deliver it to me.

The book is an ugly awful orange, clothbound and oddly vertically oversized. It is very plain. It is set like a dissertation in careful double-spaced Courier. It is 444 pages long. It looks exactly as if it were published in 1974, which in fact it was. What I love most about this book is that it begins with such a fantastic first sentence to its preface. The strength of this opening compels me to read (without much, if any, understanding) from the book at least once a month. This sentence of course is blatantly self-evident as an introduction to any book of nonfiction, but is also so brilliantly observant that I truly believe there is some vital truth still awaiting me in the impenetrable heart of the book. That sentence is:

"Very few of the remarks I could make about this book would be helpful to those who have not yet read the book."

That carries a sense of absolute logic in action. And it is this defeated compulsive dedication to honesty that I'm sure is the best quality I have inherited from my parents. Both are pessimists of a joyful sort, standard for logician atheists, although one is deeply empathic and one is deeply detached. My father in particular is in love with this sort of failure.

I was raised by my mother, but I spent a few hot central California summers with my father while I was 9, 10, and 11. While my father and stepmother were off milking the goats on their farm on the grounds of the state mental hospital for the criminally insane, I would practice the logic exercises left to me for entertainment and education. In those days most of my real life took place deep in my muddled interior: outwardly I mostly remember being confused and irrational, and always sleepy, and bizarrely resistant to any sort of discipline. I remember most that I was an element of disorder in my father's household. I annoyed the herding dog, I didn't know how to cook from Julia Child, I lied to my stepmother, and I was expensive. Worst of all, these exercises presented as games baffled me.

Beneath my window in my part-time bedroom a massive mint bush sprawled; out beyond that was the barn where the food animals were slit open as they hung from hooks in their ankles, beyond that the sheep pasture, and then the 101 freeway. Staring out at that and beyond in the dry afternoons, I'd try to learn the order of the Greek alphabet and fail. I'd try to learn number-ordering games, logical exclusion games, riddles, and fallacies. Nothing seemed to penetrate. I absorbed nothing and felt like a fool. I realized that my parents' theoretical world was not for me, and in a combination of rebellion and self-sabotage I promptly made a desperate attempt to fail eighth grade. Not long thereafter I graduated high school in the top 70 percent of my class and refused to even apply to college.

Yet to this day one working remnant of my flawed education is my ingrained sixth sense for fallacy. Fallacious thinking upsets me irrationally in myself and in others, and every day I strive to strip these ugly reminders of failure from my speech and acts. That was my father's gift. Well: that, and a natural and profitable ease with the applied mathematics of gambling.

Shortly after high school, after I had stopped talking to my father and my stepmother, over nothing much really, a minor altercation, mostly a realization that I barely knew them and didn't share much with them, my father sent my mother a letter in which he expressed his disappointment with me and in which he used the phrase "filial piety."

This so encapsulated my experience with my father the logician that I laughed and laughed at the letter, even as it upset me, and even as I knew his point was absolutely accurate; that sons have duties to their fathers no matter what their situations. I was not ready to make contact with him at the time, due to various personal messinesses of my life, and now the years have flown by with a failure on my part to take any corrective action whatsoever. This is where logic fails us.

Site: Choire Sicha Dot Com

URL: http://choiresicha.com

When The Waiter Came...

Wil Wheaton

The plan was to meet Anne and the girls at The Cheesecake Factory, but I guess the wait there was 45-70 minutes. 45-70 minutes?! Does anyone really want to wait that long for a seat in a restaurant? Sure, at Hooters I can understand that, but at The Cheesecake Factory?

I guess the girls all felt the same way, so they went to some place called "Champps Americana", which is sort of a sportsbar/micro-brewery/ I'm-having-a-mid-life-crisis-and-I-want-to-eat-at-a-place-like-the-ones-I-went-to-in-college place.

So we get seated, and we're ordering, and, right in the middle of Anne giving her order, the waiter cuts her off, points towards me, and says, "Hey! The kid from Stand By Me!" Now, whenever that happens, I don't quite know what to say. Should I jump up and shout "Traaiiiiinnnn!" or tell him a story, or what? I never know how to handle that...I don't want to say, "Yes! You are correct, sir! Now please treat me differently the entire course of our meal, for I am from movies!". So there's this tiny, uncomfortable pause, and my friend Stephanie follows the waiter's pointing finger, over my shoulder and says, 'You know, I think that is Corey Feldman, right over there!" And we all laughed, and it was okay.

So we're waiting for our dinner to come, and waiting, and waiting, and getting hungrier and hungrier, and this runner finally comes by with some food. He sets Steph's ribs down in front of her, and as he's leaning over, he dumps a huge, Ron Jeremy-sized load of alfredo juice all down the shoulder and back of my cool fairview t-shirt! Suddenly, he realizes two things: The food is not ours, it goes to the table next to us, and he just spooged pasta sauce all over my back. So what does he do? He picks up the ribs, says NOTHING about my back! Nothing at all! Not even, "sorry" or "who's your daddy, Wesley?"

So this is a huge mess down my back, and it takes two napkins to wipe it all off...and Stephanie says, "The least he could have done is bought you dinner before he came on your back." And my wife says, "Yeah, now you are totally his bitch."

I realize that some of you are having your image of sweet little Gordie and uber-square Wesley completely shattered right now, but I think it's best that you get to know the real me sooner than later, that way it won't hurt so badly when we break up.

Okay, back to the story: FINALLY, our food comes, and it is brought to us by the manager. So I see this guy in a tie coming over, and I think, "Sweet! This turkey burger is on the house!"

He sets our food down, apologizes for the wait, and leaves!! He doesn't even acknowledge the stain down my back! Now, maybe he didn't know....I can't imagine this conversation:

Runner: Uh, sir? I just came on the back of TV's Wil Wheaton

Manager: Good job, Darryl! I always hated Wesley Crusher anyway!

But you know what I really think? I think the huge, corporate, "sportsbar/ micro-brewery/I'm-having-a-mid-life-crisis-and-I-want-to-eat-at-a-place-like-the-ones-I-went-to-in-college place" doesn't care about your Uncle Willie, and you know why? Because he isn't the target audience. He wasn't wearing penny loafers without socks and corduroy shorts. He didn't have a ponytail, and he wasn't drinking Smirnoff Ice when the Zima ran out!!

Oh well. The food wasn't too bad, and the waitstaff did come and sing "Happy Birthday" to my wife...and our waiter was pretty cool...he could keep up with our sarcasm and jokes and stuff...Oh, and there were lots of interesting people to watch while we ate...which reminds me, and get out a pencil and write this down, people: Just because they make a babydoll t-shirt that says "sexy" in rhinestone across the chest in a size 18 doesn't mean anyone should wear it! Because, damn, man, dimples, okay? Okay.

Site: Wil Wheaton Dot Net

URL: http://wilwheaton.net

I Saw U

Matthew Baldwin

Defective Yeti

I saw U Thurs. at Sam's Bar & Grill. Me: blond, blue eyes, jeans, Hooters t-shirt, approached and suggested that we go to my place so you could check out my hard drive. You: pretty, petite, dark hair, reading "Underworld", said you'd rather eat a thumbtack sandwich than go home with me. I didn't get your number. Call me, drinks? 5099

Site: Defective Yeti

URL: http://www.defectiveyeti.com

Red Hot And Blue

Janet Feeney

I woke up with a mean case of the blues this morning. I should have seen it coming, since I stayed up ridiculously late last night, a technique I have used since I was a little girl: since tomorrow comes fast once you're asleep, you can slow it down if you never get to bed.

The jobless thing is getting to me, bad. I think I gave myself mental permission to chill out until summer was over, and guess what. I've at least been lucky enough to discuss a number of promising opportunities but so far nothing has turned into something concrete. I'm trying to not get excited about a "let's talk" anymore. Although I do, and then I feel like crap when it doesn't pan out.

My bank account is dwindling at an alarming rate, which is going to force me to take drastic action soon. I know, I know: everything will sort itself out. I'm reminding myself that the bad feeling in the pit of my stomach is a tremendous motivator.

Speaking of the economy, I missed Bush's appeal for $87 billion dollars last night. When I read the synopsis on CNN last night, I immediately pictured Tim Robbins in *Austin Powers* laughing at Dr. Evil's ransom demand for a "million kajillion dollars" $87 billion—why it's such an odd number? Clearly, Iraq will be a huge money drain for many years to come. We all knew that going in (or should have).

Keep in mind $87 billion is on TOP of the Outstanding Public Debt that as of 08 Sep 2003 at 03:38:24 PM GMT is $6,818,293,305,301 or $23,353.85 per person. If one more smug Republican tells me the Democrats are the tax and spend party, I'm going to slug him in the face. The "tax cut no matter what" Republican fiscal management under this Administration is unforgivable.

Of course, the need for so much money implies the continuing cost of human lives. We're there, and we need to do what it takes. I get it. I'm not arguing for pulling out—heaven forbid. (Although I heard my first pundit—Carnegie president Jessica Mathews—argue for it on Thursday's *Charlie Rose* show.) But once again, Bush's speech wraps everything up in the righteous war on terror, providing no details, no timelines, no accountability. Just trust that they will do the right thing. Mr. Bush, I would like nothing more. But I can't.

I was against this war from the beginning, not because I am a pacifist, but because I found the Bush administration's entire march to war self-serving and shortsighted. Winning the war: can be done at some hard cost. Winning the peace: unbelievably hard, long and expensive with a high likelihood of failure with the best planning and intentions. It's the lack of a credible dialogue on winning the peace that made me oppose the invasion.

I just reread what I posted last February, in the weeks leading to the war, and I have seen no evidence that would convince me to change what I wrote then: "It is not un-American to think our foreign policy at the moment is a depressing combination of self-serving spin supporting bluntly self-serving actions that are more closely tied to short-term political ambition than a long-range, coherent construction of policy in the region. It's realistic."

Don't get me wrong. 9/11 was a drastic call to action. Force and sacrifice are required. I do worry about missing the forest for the trees. If one of the points of invading Iraq is to develop a swatch of the Middle East that we can control instead of relying so heavily on the "are-they or aren't-they implicated in 9/11" Saudis, I can understand that. I'd be happier arguing real strategic goals than enduring the constantly evolving "sales pitch for war": Iraq is synonymous with al Qaeda; Hussein has weapons of mass destruction; we are liberators freeing an oppressed people. The fact that the spin changes so much makes me distrust all of their rhetoric.

I read that Bush said last night: "We have learned that terrorist attacks are not caused by the use of strength; they are invited by the perception of weakness. And the surest way to avoid attacks on our own people is to engage the enemy where he lives and plans. We are fighting that enemy in Iraq and Afghanistan today so that we do not meet him again on our own streets, in our own cities."

I cannot agree more. I support this idea fully. Isn't this similar to the aftermath of Pearl Harbor and Germany's subsequent declaration of war on the US in 1941? The goals of our foreign policy should be a no-brainer. Beat the bad guy. But when I think about how we're going about it, something doesn't feel right.

The administration has already admitted their post-invasion scenario theories did not match anything close to reality; that we need the help of the entire world (let's hope our fellow democracies agree to our new demands and that "paying for the war with oil money" remains a wonderful pipe dream (pun intended) that equates to me solving my current problems by winning the lottery (even American-in-charge Paul Bremer has moved off this). The debate over the number and duration of military deployments remains a painful, hotly argued topic.

And then there are the whispers about ties between the Bushes, the oil industry, the bin Laden family and the Saudi government, implying a massive conflict of interest.Who knows what the truth is there.

Full disclosure: my misgivings about our direction in Iraq are directly affected by what I consider to be the Republican assault on democracy in the United States. The Texas redistricting grab and the recall election in California, both examples of Republicans bolstering power through seizure rather than the regular electoral/judicial process.

But wait, there's more. The pandering to big business is appalling. The rollback of decades of environmental protection laws to suit big-donating corporations. The failure to adjudicate corporate crimes like the Enron fraud. Republican-led energy deregulation as the root cause of the power failures in California and the Northeast.

The shameless use of terror to support partisan politics. The late date of the Republican National Convention (August 30–September 2) next year in New York City, the first time that city has hosted them in their 147 year history (cue shameless use of 9/11 memorializing for political gain).

And on and on.

Every time I write a post like this, I get a sickening image of my file on John Ashcroft's database growing a little fatter. Because they need to keep track of people like me. Think I'm paranoid? Go rent *Watch on the Rhine* and compare current events with the movie's descriptions of the rise of European and Japanese fascism that lead to World War II. Mind you, George W. Bush does not even belong in the same sentence with Hitler. What I'm comparing is how people in power can use a combination of fear, intimidation and coddling the egos of the masses to their advantage in advancing a highly personal agenda.

Which brings me to the upcoming 9/11 anniversary this week, which has suddenly begun to hang over me like a pall. I deleted all the World Trade Center programming my TiVo so helpfully suggested. Watching all the memorials last year was very traumatizing in its own way, although devoting an entire evening to expressing my grief proved therapeutic.

Instead, my observance will be spent in a jury room. I have to serve Wednesday / Thursday, unless I get a trial or am dismissed. Voting and jury duty are my only civic duties (since I'm unlikely to be drafted); and as flawed as the system is, American justice is one of the foundations of the American republic.

So I'll go and hope I don't have to do anything except show up—can't get more American than that. I'll see the deformed skyline from Jersey City and once again wonder if I dreamed those two buildings rising into the sky. Until I meet someone who lost someone that day, or cares for someone who was hurt, or who lives with the knowledge that it could have been them. And then I'll remember it as one of the realest days of my life.

That's the worst thing that can happen, isn't it. Not being alone, or broke, or up to eyeballs in debt, or frustrated, or permanently appalled by my country's actions, although I live with the possibility of all of them coming true.

What I really fear is that I, or someone I love, will be murdered in an unbelievably brutal way because of greed, of fanaticism, of ideas. In my heart, I've accepted that the next attack is coming. I'm not alone: according to *Time,* 72% of Americans expect another terrorism attack within the next year. But what would wake me up (if I ever went to bed) is that a failure to successfully rebuild Iraq and Afghanistan will act like a terrorism Miracle-Gro.

Site: Snarkcake

URL: http://www.snarkcake.com

Interview with Janet Feeney of Snarkcake

Writer Janet Feeney may be a self-employed marketing communications specialist by day, but in her off hours, her blog Snarkcake takes on a life of its own. Writing about everything from terrorist attacks to the most annoying contestant on *Survivor*, Feeney has a knack for showing fellow bloggers an interesting cross-section of American culture.

Why is your blog called Snarkcake?

I was inspired by a long-running joke on *The X-Files* boards at Television Without Pity (www.televisionwithoutpity.com). During the summer before the show's last season, the last of us diehard fans were lamenting the rapidly diminishing quality of a once brilliant show. We wished that someone would stick a pointy stick in Chris Carter's bicycle wheel to incapacitate him for a little while—maybe someone else would produce the show for a while and we'd get back some plot continuity or characters we recognized. Someone posted that she would spring the guilty party from jail with a cunning use of snark and a cake with a file in it. And a website was named that day.

It's fitting that those boards were the source of my blog's name. I found sites like Television Without Pity after I was laid off in the fall of 2000 and I was blown away at how many smart people were out there who were as obsessed with pop culture as I was. Participating in those forums gave me some of the confidence I needed to put my opinions out on my own site.

Why did you feel compelled to write about your experiences online?

My dear friend Freakgirl (www.freakgirl.com) has been blogging since 1999 and I thought it was so cool. When I realized I was sending her stuff for her blog a few times a week, it dawned on me that I should get my own. Most of my posts are comments about life as we know it—entertainment, politics, silly news stories, issues that effect people I know. Once in a while I write something personal about myself, but almost always springing from some other context. I would never publish a journal—my life is not interesting enough to dissect on a regular basis. I also don't write about anything I wouldn't want my friends or family to know—I assume they all read my blog, so I would never publish something I wouldn't talk about in the real world.

Blogging is like a great cocktail party conversation online. Sometimes it's serious, sometimes it's light as air—it depends on what is the topic of the day. In the real world, I'm the funny woman at the party with all the weird trivia—when my friends need to settle a bet on who sang "Billy Don't Be a Hero," I get the call. So my blog is the written version of what I might chatter about whilst balancing a glass and a plate.

The truth is that big media pays as much attention to Britney Spears' quickie marriage as it does to rebuilding Afghanistan. All of that stuff fits into our public discourse, so my blog tends to reflect whatever the focus of the moment is, rather than a specific theme.

The big bonus is being a part of a community of very smart people that share a critical love for the silly things like Robbie Williams and "Survivor" but also a concern for life and death issues such as terrorism and AIDS. We are not alone.

What has the reaction been from people regarding your blog? What did you learn from the experience?

I was so nervous when I started—I had so much admiration for so many other blogs and wasn't sure I was good enough. It was thrilling to hear from people whose blogs I had followed for a year who would write to say they enjoyed my site.

I still get puzzled looks from family and friends who are not active in the online world. I've been asked everything from "What's snark?" (A: a combo of snide and sarcastic), "What's a blog?" to "What's in it for you?" It's made me very aware of the divide between those of us who have seized the chance to get into the discourse online and those who are not interested in that at all.

Blogging introduced me to the thoughts and opinions of other cool people I never would have met otherwise. It's a rich, robust source for content not dependent on pleasing advertisers or dictated by the politics of big media. It's personal, unfiltered, and for now at least, real.

Blogging also made me write every day—write for myself, not for work. At first, I was concerned I couldn't make the commitment to generating content day after day. But I really enjoy it—most of what I write about is rattling around my head anyway. I think that posting something every day—even if I just compose a sentence or two—has improved my writing. I now have the courage to say, "I'm a writer."

Do you read other people's online journals?

My daily reads include the folks I feel are the equivalent of the kids you sat with at lunch in high school. Freakgirl (www.freakgirl.com), Unsided (www.unsided.com), JohnnyaGoGo (www.johnnyagogo.com), and Atilla's Litterbox (http://www.atilla.demon.nl/blogger.html). With the exception of Freakgirl, whom I've known for a while, I've met all of these people—online and then in person—since I launched Snarkcake. The Web brought us together.

Why do you think blogging has become so popular in the last few years?

The same reason amateur moviemakers rejoiced at the dawn of the camcorder—affordable publishing technology has enabled us to practice our art even if we're not professionals. Finally, people who want to write for a hobby or who aspire to write professionally can get read. Before the Internet, I had friends who self-published fanzines that have to be passed as an object in the real world. That's a level of commitment I never would have made—but I can commit to five links a day, then click Rebuild.

I think when this era is looked back on, it will be seen as a great age for essays, commentary, and nonfiction—and blogs will have played a big part of that. It's the Diary of Samuel Pepys times a million voices (he's got a blog too—http://pepysdiary.com/).

What do you hope people learn about you from your writing?

I hope they are entertained—that's the goal. Once in a while, for example on World AIDS Day, I hope that I can share information that promotes awareness or gives people food for their thought as they form their own opinions about the world. In the days leading up to the Iraq war, many of my posts were more political than usual because that what my focus was. I felt proud that discussion on my site was international, that in a very, very small way, I contributed my point of view to the discourse and some folks found it meaningful and they added their own point of view—and I learned from it when they did not agree, too.

I am knowable through what I choose to post, but I prefer to remain fairly anonymous about who I am in the real world. I like the freedom of having a voice distinct from my true identity. It's probably some leftover superhero fantasy—by day, mild mannered marketing writer, by night astute commentator on what to watch, who to vote for, and what's going on in the world. Plus there's no silly costume to dry clean.

I've had a lot of personal and professional ups and downs over the past few years, so I'm enjoying the lull at the moment. But if the Pixies reunite, we could be looking at a banner year.

Disasters Of The Natural Variety

Heather B. Armstrong

Yesterday morning at approximately 9:30 am PST, a smallish rumbling earthquake hit Los Angeles and woke me from a drooling slumber. It was the first earthquake I've ever been awake or sober enough to experience, and like any other natural disaster frightened me into rabid cable news channel surfing and knuckle gnawing for the rest of the afternoon.

Rounding out the list of phobias that render me a paralyzed, shivering goose bump—fear of heights, rodents, spiders, and hairy toes to name just a few—is a mammoth anxiety over potential natural disasters, thoroughly aggravated in my youth by my older brother's daily tortuous threat: "Do what I say or the tornado will come and get you."

Tornado season in Tennessee starts in mid-March and continues through July, sometimes hiccupping into the latter part of September. When thunderstorms aren't uprooting forests or rearranging acres of farmland, the South often suffers hailstorms, flashfloods and torrentially ghoulish winds during this season. Rarely is there a week not littered with severe thunderstorm warnings blinking in red Helvetica across the bottom of *Days Of Our Lives.*

In the Spring of 1983 on a seemingly innocuous March afternoon, I was making dirt and grass soup with a fellow eight year old neighbor when a warning siren sounded four blocks away at the local fire station. To my little third grade ears, it sounded like one of them there 18 wheelers we done seen on the highway when we would go visit granny in Kentucky and eat fried chicken with our fangers. Blissfully unaware of the pending tornado extravaganza, I quietly noted the passing truck and went back to picking rocks out of my mud soup.

Within one minute of its first pass, however, that there big truck done come back around and passed again. Then again within another minute. On its eighth pass I figured the truck just couldn't remember where it done needed to be! And by this time every single resident of Cedar Oak Cove had gathered into a huddled mass of wonder in the middle of the street, staring up into the orange glow of oncoming clouds. Because, you see, that's what Southerners do when faced with a plausibly disastrous situation: they gonna get themselves front row seats! And thus we have NASCAR.

After gathering enough information to piece together that it was in fact a tornado warning and that my neighborhood sat directly in the path of the red splotches on the radar screen, I spent the next seven years locked in my bathroom with all my stuffed animals, sleeping in the bathtub with my favorite pillow and a bucket of Cheez-its.

Eighteen years later and over 1000 miles from any weather conducive to tornado formation, I've got earthquakes to worry about and no siren-ific warnings or radar screens to issue me into the tub and into safety. I wonder how long I can stand under a doorframe before passing out.

Site: Dooce

URL: http://dooce.com

September 11, 2003

Choire Sicha

Armistice Day, the 11th of November, was recognized by Congress in 1926 as a remembrance of the date of the end of "the most destructive, sanguinary, and far reaching war in human annals." Now become Veteran's Day, it's a day for Jay Leno jokes about Vietnam vets.

In 1872, Julia Ward Howe began to advocate for the idea of an annual Mother's Day as a protest against warmakers' slaughter of their sons. By now, Mother's Day is for most a guilty Hallmark moment of recompense.

Since Labor Day's invention as a celebration of unions and workers in 1882, it has come to mean lawn parties and the stowing of white shoes. Solemn Decoration Day became bar-be-que sauce Memorial Day, and the crucifixion of Christ on Easter has become a day of bunnies and peeps, and, queerly, egg hunting.

And what will we do to September 11th in a hundred years? Will New Yorkers put little aluminum twin towers in their living rooms, with little presents underneath? An empty table setting at the picnic table, like Elijah's? Will it be an official bank-closing holiday? Will the federal government take it for their National Anti-Terrorism Day? Will suburban children race about their Westchester lawns with toy jets, shrieking "I'm going to fly a plane into you?" Or will the random intrude: will we make little Arab terrorist masks and go trick-or-treating?

The human—or maybe American—capacity for refusing to retain any focus on disaster or grief with any dignity or sense is historically absolutely unlimited. Two years later, the remembrance of September 11th is already a day of frothy emotional appeal: children's faces in the World Trade Center pit, a day when we set aside squabbles over multi-million dollar celebrity architects' contracts and multi-billion dollar insurance lawsuits. It is a day of grotesquery without any relation to actual horror or content. Already September 11th has become a day when we must put critical thought on hold and pretend to focus on the public's morass of feelings. From the substance of those feelings, or from the skewed re-weaving of the media's representations of those feelings, inexcusable foreign and domestic policies are enacted. That use of September 11th is perhaps most offensive of all, and it is what will predominate as September 11th is drained of any particular meaning it might have had—might have had—in the decades to come.

Site: Choire Sicha Dot Com

URL: http://choiresicha.com

Business Cards

Greg Apt

I always carry cards around, and I give them to my clients liberally. Why? It's a sort of funny story, but it goes back to when I first became a PD and was so happy to have a real job that I could put "Attorney at Law" on my cards, that I got them right away. Many PDs I knew never got cards, saying that the last thing they needed was their names getting around the jail.

Well, I got cards, and when I first started out arraigning people ("these are the charges against you, you'll have a prelim/trial in so many days, what happened," etc..., but no real legal work) I would often have clients ask for a card. Knowing that I was not going to represent them any further, I still gave them cards. You wouldn't believe the buzz that went on in lockup after that happened. The client I gave the card to would go back into lockup and show it to someone else and say something to the effect of "look at what I got, my lawyer's a real lawyer, he gave me a card." The others would gather around, and then begin badgering me to represent them too.

Did it make a difference in my representation of them? You bet. As I have mentioned, people frequently (and incorrectly) think that us PDs are crappy lawyers, and that we're trying to dump them. Little things can dispel notions like this. One of those things are cards, it makes us look more professional. It may not help with every client, but it certainly helps a lot. Now, every time I meet a client for the first time, I give him or her a card, as if I was a high priced private lawyer meeting a well-paying client for the first time over a $300 dinner. It makes a huge difference, especially to someone who is suspicious that he is having some loser lawyer thrown at him for the sole purpose of getting him to plead guilty and go to jail for a long time.

The lesson: always look and act as professional as you can. It doesn't mean that you can't be a rebel (for many years I've worn an earring in Court), but it means that you exude confidence and competence, and people will believe it—even juries, all of which really matters.

Site: Public Defender Dude

URL: http://publicdefenderdude.blogspot.com/

Jury Duty

Janet Feeney

Jury duty was not what I expected. Not at all. This is my third go-round in the Hudson County Superior Court on jury duty, so I thought I had the routine down pat.

I arrived at 8:40 for the 8:30 report time (although nothing gets going until 9AM so I wasn't concerned about the ten minutes). The jury room was already packed full—there were easily 300 people with plenty of later arrivals still in line behind me.

My fellow jury pool comrades were a walking commercial for diversity. There was every skin tone, age and stereotype from white wannabe-rapper teens to high-powered black businesswomen. I felt very proud that all of these different faces from every part of the globe were American, that we were all part of the same process.

At 9, as usual, the announcements start. But this time instead of a general overview of "what it means to be a juror," the manager comes out and gives very detailed instructions about how we have to report back if the judges excuse us, how we will be hunted down if cigarette/potty breaks exceed 20 minutes, etc. So I knew I was in for something more involved than I had experienced previously. Must be a murder, or some major organized crime case.

Then the woman ahead of me mentioned there was a death penalty case seating jurors that was in the Jersey City paper yesterday. And my jaw hit the floor. I saw another juror, a professional-looking white man in his 40s, blanch when he heard her.

We were prospective jurors in a death penalty case.

I started chatting with the guy to my left about previous jury bouts. He'd been called twice before in NYC and this was his first time in NJ. He was confident he wouldn't make the jury since "his parents are lawyers and I don't believe in the death penalty under any circumstances." I complimented him on the firmness of his beliefs.

Inside, I was both impressed and annoyed by the strengths of his convictions. As I mulled, I realized that I probably could never vote for the death penalty. Although maybe I could. Could I? What if it were one of my family members or friends? What if it were one of the serial killers from all those true crime books I read on vacation? Believe me, the irony was not lost on me.

I probably agreed with him—why is everything such a struggle with me? Probably because the "right thing" is so elusive...what is right according to the dead man's family, to the accused's family, to the police, to society, to my religious upbringing? Gah.

Back to the procedural. First came a massive role call like taking attendance of the whole school on the first day back. Then 150 of us were to be randomly grouped into units of 25 to take the elevators to the 9th floor. I was the first person in the second to last group called.

The courtroom was already full of jurors and I found an odd seat toward the front. The people who came in last sat in the jury box or stood. I craned to get a look at the defendants. There were 5 people at the defense table, all in suits, so I wasn't sure who were the attorneys, who were the defendants. Who looked like a murderer? Have I ever seen one with my own eyes before?

Could I imagine pointing at one of them and saying, "You shall die for your crimes." Would I feel differently when I heard the evidence, saw the family crying, heard fellow police officers demand the ultimate punishment?

The judge began by explaining that this was a criminal case and the jury selection was not going to be typical. I think I was still in denial. He started reading the indictment to us. When the defendant's names were read, half the courtroom gasped. My sinking feeling sunk lower.

Then he said it: "This is a capital case." It was real. My head swam. I felt nauseous. My hands were sticky. The air left the room. All I could think was, "I can't handle the stress of deliberating and unanimously agreeing with 11 other people over a murder, let alone a police officer's murder, let alone decide whether someone should die for his crimes." I took a deep breath and tried to focus on what the judge was saying. Just listen to the words, one by one.

I started to relax a bit. Certainly, I thought, my doubts as to whether I could administer the death penalty will surely disqualify me. And I started thinking about the odds. 18 out of 600...

After a lengthy reading of the crimes, the potential witnesses and the whole "innocent until proven guilty" instructions, the judge said that he expected the trial to begin in early October and would run approximately six–eight weeks. Another audible gasp went up from the jurors. The next step was for all of us to complete a questionnaire and we would be asked to return at some point next week for individual interviews. Unless we couldn't serve the length of the trial.

Eight weeks. On some level, I have the time. It would be fascinating. It would be the most important thing I had ever done. But could I handle the stress of coming to a unanimous conclusion. I didn't think so—and I don't think so sitting here writing this, days later.

And then the hammer fell. "Your attitudes about the death penalty are not an excuse. The fact you are needed at work is not an excuse. The only excuses I want to hear are about why you cannot serve. You know a witness, you would be financially damaged because you work for pay or you're unemployed, you're having surgery, are a caregiver for a dependent, or you're getting married." Unbelievably, a glimmer shone from my personal darkness. Damned unemployment was about to save me.

I watched as about half the group stood to move on to the questionnaire. Both the woman who first intimated it was a death penalty case and the man who blanched left the room. They were moving on. "No death penalty guy" stayed with me.

Each hopeful reject was called one by one to speak to the judge and the attorneys to either be excused or sent to the questionnaire room. It was the ultimate trip to the principal's office; instead of detention and a note on your permanent record, the worst that could happen was a fine and a possible jail sentence for refusing to cooperate.

The Parade of Stereotypes filed up one by one. Many were from the same fold: the single parents, folks with concerns about their English proficiency, the large brigade of self-employed, freelancing or unemployed white collars, the blue collars without a decent leave policy. Like a *Seinfeld* episode, a few stood out:

The guy with the Dying Fetus t-shirt. I couldn't hear him, but I was amused to see the prosecutor reading the tour dates on the back of his shirt with a bemused smile while he spoke to the judge. Maybe they are on tour this fall? Given that three recent Dying Fetus tracks are "Blunt Force Trauma," "Beaten Into Submission," and "Nothing Left To Pray For," I doubt he would have gotten past the questionnaire anyway.

The cranky elderly man in the apple green Mr. Rogers sweater who complained to the sheriff about the order in which we were being called to see the judge. He turned to me indignantly to complain that this process was worse than the Army. I was too afraid of further contact to do anything than noncommittally agree. When he finally saw the judge just before lunch break, the conversation was lengthy and he was one of about 5 people sent on to the questionnaire instead of being excused. I guess he wanted his hearing.

The Hispanic stylist guy and the Asian low-talking cost accountant guy I hung out with in the hall during the break; all strangers willing to share intimate details of our lives; who is taking a dream trip to Hawaii, where are the best places we've traveled, who is having surgery, who has a hearing problem, who is working, who isn't working.

I had lunch with a very nice woman, a fellow web freelancer, ostensibly networking but confiding to each other how our views on jury duty were shaped by 9/11, which led to the "what's your 9/11" story that witnesses always share. Our perfect view of Ground Zero after lunch was all too fitting.

Although I rehearsed my spiel to the judge in my head a million times, I was not very graceful or articulate when I got up there (for example, I didn't answer right away when he asked me what I did for a living.) But I got my point across and I was free. My new freelance friend and I headed back to the jury room, were dismissed for good about 15 minutes later and walked to Journal Square to return home.

Suddenly, I thought of us as a cast on a reality show, "This is the true story of 12 strangers, picked to serve on a jury, and have their lives taped. Find out what happens when the death penalty stops being an abstract concept and starts getting real."

Far, far too real for me. I said a heartfelt thank you to The Powers That Be for sparing me.

And a prayer on behalf of the victims, the families, the attorneys, the litigants and the jurors-to-be who weren't so lucky.

Site: Snarkcake

URL: http://snarkcake.com

Poll: 7/5 of Americans Don't Bother To Do The Math

Matthew Baldwin

A new poll shows that seven out of every five of Americans don't bother to do the math. "When asked, 53% percent said that, when reading or hearing anything that involves two or more numbers, they don't even try to do the math," said lead pollster Bradley Noel. "Another 49% said they will often think about doing the math but ultimately decide against it. Only 19% said they will actually add things up to see if the report makes sense." The results were greeted with elation from the 47 Republicans and 38 Democrats in the 100-member Senate. "This is great news," said Senate Majority Leader Pam Crader(D). "When discussing budgets or taxes, we can pretty much make stuff up: millions, trillions, deficits, surpluses—it's all the same to them." Advertisers were equally enthusiastic. "This will allow us to offer consumers 1500 free hours of service during their first month of membership," said AOL marketer Ted Rawlins. Only the Department of Education has expressed misgivings about the findings. "Mathematical apathy is one of the top three educational problems this nation faces," DOE Chairman David Kahn warned. "The other one is illiteracy."

Site: Defective Yeti

URL: http://www.defectiveyeti.com

Chatty

Allison Lowe

I am having one of those weeks where I just want to update Hate Your Daddy (HYD) every day. I don't have that much to talk about, really, but several times a day, I have wished I could sling out a mini-entry or two about the minutia of my goings on. What happens is, I get started on an entry, and it gets annoying and I don't have time to edit it, so I haven't updated a single time. The irony is thick, Alanis.

Really, right now I just want to tell someone, besides the unfortunate, beleagured people in my life who already have to hear about it everyday, about this project I am currently editing which is 30 pages of the most boring stuff about occupational health you have ever even imagined. I know. You don't imagine things like that. Anyway, it's awful. The title: "Cost Benefit and Cost Effectiveness Analysis." I just spent an hour trying to track down a style rule about whether or not any of those words should be hyphenated. Did I mention that I don't really get paid enough for this job? "Is there enough money in the world, Al?" you ask. You know the answer is "no," and that is why you are my favorite.

See, I'm already off-track here, which is just going to prove the futility of this experiment. Y'all know pamie and her friend Dan have started "blogging," right? stee has a new one, too. C. Yarbrough? A blogger. Jessica Harbour? Blogs. Omar, blogging everywhere. These are all people I love and respect, but...Frankly, I find the use of the word "blog" to be unforgivable. Web Log. Web log. Weblog. Blog. In all forms, it combines sounds that lovers of the English language feel should not be combined. I'm a fan of the purported ease with which a person can supposedly update one of those things—in all honesty, it is the laborious process of updating HYD that keeps me from doing it more frequently—but I cannot get behind the modernity of the look and feel of a blog. I don't like them. In my opinion, they are the video that is killing the radio star of good online journal writing. Yes, my friends, we've reached that point in history where someone can feel nostalgic about the good old days of the Internet.

And now I seem to be writing a whole journal entry about how I am thinking of starting a blog, and I am talking myself out of it, at length, before your very eyes. People, it could not get anymore "real time" around here.

What does one say in a blog? Am I legally obligated to link to news items? If so, I will have to start reading the news.

Can I just tell you a funny story that happened the other night? See, if this was a journal entry, that would be no big deal, but if I am supposed to be "web logging," and I don't actually log anything, I will feel like a hoax.

Forget it, mayn. I can't have a blog. All day long it will be entries like this:

9:30 a.m

Chris told me last night that he loves me "more than he used to." Haaaaa. I think he was going for that sentiment "more today than yesterday, and less than tomorrow," or whatever it is, but still—so funny.

9:47 a.m

Why the hell does it take Anna Beth so long to answer an e-mail?

9:51 a.m

I just told Hannah that "arguing with the Chris is like arguing with all four heads of Mt. Rushmore." Still laughing at my own joke.

10:23 a.m.

My boss just came in and asked me to read a two million page article about asbestos.

10:24 a.m.

zzzzzz...should I get a hair cut?

I don't think I'll do it. If I updated too much, woudln't I lose that mysterious quality you all have come to love? I'm not mysterious, am I? I'll think about it. I don't know. Can I call it something else? Can I coin a term that means journal-like blog, or weblog-like journal? Journog? Webnal? Help me!

Ponder that, readers. Meanwhile, I will go and sharpen my pencil for page two of the "Ccossszzzzzzz..."

Site: Hate Your Daddy

URL: http://hateyourdaddy.com

Look On The Bright Side

Heather B. Armstrong

I'm really just about up to here with people who tell me, "Look at it this way, at least you can write about it on your website!" and then smile as if they've made it all better. It seems that as long as I have a website, I can't really have a bad day, because a bad day only means great content. Who wants to read about someone else's good day anyway? Like, who wants to read about some dimpled-face motherfucker walking on sunshine when you just woke up and realized that your pants will no longer zip up over your thighs?

Recently I have been living great content. It goes without saying that living with your parents provides nothing but volumes of self-help memoir material, mostly in the vein of How To manuals, like: "How to Avoid Running into Granny While She's Wearing Nothing But Her Heavenly Underwear: A Former Mormon's Guide to Dealing With A Fanatical Family" or "How to Piss Off Your Step-Father Every Single Second of the Day, Volume One: It All Starts With Stealing His Razor to Shave Your Legs."

Other recent grumbles that make better stories than actual events to live through:

****

I agree to go to the grocery store for Aunt Lola, who is currently suffering from a wild strain of pneumonia, and when I show up she has this "list" ready for me, only this "list" resembles not so much a list but a 400 page Masters thesis on brand awareness. It takes me three hours of roaming around a Walmart Superstore in the most depressing neighborhood of Salt Lake City to find the specific green bag of Country Cousins Sausage she must have in order for her "bowels to be gettin' back to normal." I cry the entire 45 minutes it takes the clerk to scan and bag all the items.

****

I wake up with a hangover, only I didn't drink the night before. I sleep the entire day and the entire next day and, not surprisingly, the entire third day. I wake up on the fourth day wearing the same flannel pajamas I was wearing the night I didn't drink.

****

All I say to the hairdresser is, "Do you think I should consider bangs?" And I know he hears me because he sort of shrugs and does this "dunno" under his breath. And three hours later after I hear the entire story of how he and his partner thought their dog was pregnant but were crushed when they learned that their pregnant dog was really just a fat dog (that fucking deceitful bitch!), I walk out of the salon with the entire front side of my hair missing. I cry the entire 30 minute drive home, wondering whether or not my husband will still love a half-bald woman, only to be locked out of the house by my step-father who really needs to forgive me for the razor thing already.

Site: Dooce

URL: http://dooce.com

Junior Crime Dog

Ali Davis

Part of my job is watching the security cameras downstairs. I have a love/hate relationship with the security cameras. Sometimes they're fun, but mostly it's a pressure situation. Nobody wants to have a box get stolen or ripped up on their shift. It's easy to keep an eye on them during slow periods, but when the register is slammed, forget it.

It's frustrating, because it's easy to tell when someone is up to no good. Thieves will come right up to the register, check a small bag, and tell you that they aren't going to steal anything. Some people give the counter a long, long look before going down, while others just try to zip past, hoping you don't see them go down at all. It's weird—people really can't seem to act normally when they're planning to be creeps. The trick, of course, is having the time to watch and catch them. Sometimes when someone's weaseling around down there, I just want to get on the Voice of God mike and say "WE CAN SEE YOU."

Winter drove me nuts because everybody dressed like a thief—bulky coats and plenty of face-covering accessories. Nowadays it's warmer (well, for Chicago) and the coat, hat, hood, scarf and sunglasses combo stands out a little more.

Not everyone that acts suspicious is going to steal or vandalize something, of course. We spent a big chunk of Saturday watching a guy down there who was hoping to masturbate. It got sort of hilarious, in a disgusting way. He would study and study the boxes, then his hand would creeeeeeep over to his crotch...and then someone would come downstairs and wreck everything.

He had dressed well for his plan, if a little obviously—a huge coat with a big, fuzzy hood, a hat pulled down over his eyes, and baggy, low-slung pants. He kept hunching away from the one security camera he'd spotted—unfortunately giving us a great face shot on the one he hadn't.

So anyway, he'd find a box that turned him on and go over to what he thought was a discreet corner, but again, we're a little high-traffic for that so he kept getting interrupted. Apparently in the old days it was different—no security cameras and longer dead spells. My manager used to clerk then, and she said that having to clean come out of the corners and off the walls was pretty routine. Now there's way less masturbating privacy, which explains the upswing in box thefts. Whackers find the image they like, but have to steal it and go somewhere else if they want an uninterrupted session. And it's pretty easy to interrupt them—all the potential jerkers I've had to deal with have been huge cowards with big shame issues. Letting them know you're on to what they're up to is usually enough to get rid of them.

Finally we got tired of our visitor and decided we'd rather roust him than catch him in the act and call the cops. (Catching a customer vandalizing, stealing, or masturbating and getting him arrested means a bonus because word gets out in the dirtball network that we prosecute. So waiting to catch a guy in the act is a temptation, but then it also carries the risk that he might finish before the police arrive.) Which meant that I got to roust him—for some reason the other people at the store, including management, have decided I'm good at flushing people out of the porn section. I'm not sure why, but I have two theories. The first is simply that I am pretty much the polar opposite of the women on the porn boxes. I don't know if I am a harsh dose of reality or if I remind them of their moms or their girlfriends or their wives or just the archetypical Feminine Principal or what, but straight guys hate it when I'm down there putting away tags. They just can't seem to deal with me, so sometimes just simply going downstairs is enough to clear the area of dirtbags and legitimate customers alike.

I do like to think I'm pretty good at it when I actually have to card them and/or ask them to leave. I try to make it a face-saving situation for everyone and acknowledge that yeah, the store's 21-and-over policy really sucks. I try to be as easygoing about it as possible, especially when I have to throw out a bunch of kids.

I get sort of conflicted about throwing kids and teenagers out of the porn section. I really don't want them down there, not because I think sex is dirty or bad, but because I don't want them to think that that's what sex is about. The stuff on our boxes is sex in the basest, sometimes most brutal terms—naked women spreading their relevant orifices and making that Porn Face. Unless you're talking about the Max Hardcore series, which involves women with "SLUT" and "WHORE" written across their foreheads in lipstick. And besides—do we really need to raise another generation of men who can't deal with pubic hair?

So I don't feel bad about getting them out of there, except that I'm very conscious of the fact that I'm a woman while I'm doing it. I worry that I'm either setting up or reinforcing the idea that there are fun, bad women who like sex and good, boring women who restrict access to sex.

I always want to debrief them. "Hey, guys, it's cool that you're curious, but this isn't the way to find out. Porn is fine, but it's not real sex. Real sex is great, and even good girls love it, but it has to be a two-way street..." But I always just end up with "Sorry, guys—come back when you're 21." Perhaps I should write a children's book. Porn Is Healthy and Fine, but Only as a Temporary Physical Release.

So anyway, I started out with the Discreet Method: I went down with a handful of tags and put away the ones right around where he was, hoping to drive him out with a quick dose of Virgin/Nun/Mom/Mother-Goddess. No dice. He just kept turning his back to me—an increasingly hard prospect as I corralled him into the corner.

He actually tried the hand creep once until he glanced over and realized I was a)an employee and b)female. He decided to wait me out, pulling his pants up and his coat down a bit—I had clearly cramped his masturbating style.

He stayed hunched in the corner and wouldn't go away on his own, so I finally broke down and asked him if he had ID and an account with us. We have a sign saying you need to set up an account to even browse down there. We don't really enforce it unless we're ousting a dirtbag, but then it comes in fairly handy. As it did in this case—just addressing him directly did the trick and he dropped his box and fled as casually as possible.

My manager high-fived me when I came up. I had kept our store clean and safe for our non-masturbating porn freaks and done my little bit to keep the virgin/whore dichotomy firmly in place.

Mom would be so proud.

Site: True Porn Clerk Stories

URL: http://www.improvisation.ws/mb/showthread.php?s=&threadid=4475

How To Annoy Me

Heather B. Armstrong

12 October 2003

I know you're fascinated with my belly button, but touch it again and you'll pull back a hand with at least three fingers missing.

23 September 2003

Continue to point out my obsessive habit of deleting shows off the TiVo. DON'T COME CRYING TO ME WHEN WE RUN OUT OF SPACE AND THE WHOLE WORLD COMES CRASHING IN.

16 September 2003

Ask me a question from the other room and keep repeating it even though I can't hear you. I know I do this, too, but it's not annoying when I do it.

05 September 2003

Try to kiss me while I'm sitting on the toilet. I know it may surprise you, but I DO have boundaries.

20 August 2003

Run inside the next door neighbor's house, eat all of their dogs' dog food, and then proceed to poop seven times in the next ten hours.

07 August 2003

Try to convince me that I should check out the new Hall and Oates cd.

05 August 2003

Call this website a "diary" or a "journal." I prefer "piece of self-loathing, self-indulgent, narcissistic crap," thank you very much.

31 July 2003

Ask me if my vagina has a monologue.

29 July 2003

During a confessional on a reality TV show use the words "connect" and "on so many levels" anywhere in the same paragraph.

25 June 2003

Sign up for a reality television show and then complain about the situations you're being put in. You'd better eat those cow intestines with a smile on your face, motherfucker.

19 June 2003

Insert the phrase "Know what I'm saying?" in between every word of a five word sentence.

17 June 2003

Think for ONE second that I won't bite your hand off if you reach over here and grab one of my french fries.

06 June 2003

Say "fetch" or "frigg" or "frick" because you don't want God to hear you say "fuck." At this point I'm pretty sure God thinks you're a fucking idiot.

02 June 2003

Try to escape the house by climbing up the built-in cabinetry, knocking out the screen to the window in the living room and perching perilously six feet above the rose bush below. You're a dog for crying out loud.

23 May 2003

Send me an email suggesting that I am a terrible person for using household cleaners on my dog. YOU don't have to live with my dog's feet.

09 May 2003

Charge me $4.50 for a cup of coffee and then tell me to put my own soy milk in it. For $4.50 you'd better be wiping my ass.

06 May 2003

Think that you can drive your car around like a total moron because you've paid your tithing and nothing bad can happen to you. News flash, buddy: I CAN HAPPEN TO YOU.

02 May 2003

Lift your right leg and pee on the new neighbor's leg.

18 April 2003

Consider yourself a better person because you don't watch "American Idol." Well, America voted, and it's official: you're a total snob.

09 April 2003

Suggest that we shouldn't let the dog sip the $39.00 Herradura tequila. You know he's totally worth it.

01 April 2003

Rip open a pink permanent marker and chew it to pieces all over my mother's immaculate beige carpet. When she sees that stain we will totally be written out of the will.

31 March 2003

Assume that Lee Greenwood has anything to do with our national anthem.

26 March 2003

Turn on a "Wiggles" video and leave me alone with your 4-yr old, you heartless, cruel monster.

25 March 2003

Smell my dog's feet and then gag loudly. What the hell did you expect, mother?

20 March 2003

Sit next to me in traffic with your windows down blasting Kenny Loggins "Danger Zone" and bop your head in rhythm with the guitar.

14 April 2002

Poop on the living room rug and then step in it.

26 March 2002

Remind me that the Easter Bunny's handwriting is remarkably similar to my father's.

19 March 2002

Jump on the bed with your big self right after I've taken the time to straighten the covers.

15 March 2002

Build a huge mall at the end of my street. This is Los Angeles, for Chrissake, not Mississippi.

08 March 2002

Ask me if I like the pantsuit you just bought on sale at Wal-Mart. I hate trick questions.

06 March 2002

Dress your dog in a sweater set and matching socks.

26 February 2002

Take an X-ray of my abdomen while whistling the chorus to a Creed song. I will see you in Hell.

Tell me that there's no good reason I should be constipated. Do I really need a good reason?

04 February 2002

Try to floss your teeth and drive at the same time. Your gingivitis can wait.

28 January 2002

Offer a six-months same as cash option on a loan. You may as well just beat me up and steal my wallet.

24 January 2002

Expect me to care about your cat. I don't.

23 January 2002

Touch my monitor with your chubby, greasy digit.

22 January 2002

Make a movie starring Kevin Costner.

21 January 2002

Use the words "Neosporin" and "sweetie" in the same sentence.

08 January 2002

Grow your sideburns into the shape and size of Louisiana. It's hurtful.

03 January 2002

Wash your car with a squeegee and two paper towels at Chevron. I thought I was white trash.

02 January 2002

Obey Utah's liquor laws and serve me only one ounce of tequila at a time. We're going to be here all night at this rate.

13 December 2001

Comment loudly at the company Christmas party, "You clean up real nice, lady."

11 December 2001

Accuse me of being pathological. My doctor calls it "terminally obsessive."

Argue that your album sold 887,000 copies in one week on its "artistic merit" alone and not because in reality you're just MTV's bitch.

28 November 2001

Tell me to stop drinking so much caffeine. You're my primary care physician, what do you know?

27 November 2001

Shave your face in the sink and leave a two-foot puddle of hairy water brimming on the countertop.

26 November 2001

Prepare a meal that sends me to sleep with 14,000 calories in my belly.

20 November 2001

Try to tell me what a girl wants. Not only are you not a girl, but you're not even Christina Aguilera.

19 November 2001

Two seconds after I point out the flab on my ass, suggest that we have brownies for breakfast.

15 November 2001

Answer the questions I ask outloud in my sleep. I'm not talking to you.

01 November 2001

Write me a ticket for going only 25 mph over the speed limit. Be glad you caught me when I was obviously sedated.

16 October 2001

After I cover one wall in thick red paint, you bump into it with your big white ass. Twice.

11 October 2001

Slow down to a complete stop at an intersection that clearly doesn't require it. Stop signs are just suggestions.

10 October 2001

Call my purse a "David Spade" bag.

04 October 2001

Ask me to shake the dew from your lily. That is just wrong. Wrong, I say.

01 October 2001

Make fun of the way I drool all over my shirt when I sleep in the car.

24 September 2001

Haggle over a women's rib-knit cowl-neck sweater that I've priced at 25 cents.

10 September 2001

Get together with your band of birds and poop all over the hood of my car.

31 August 2001

Make me pack in an orderly fashion. I just don't have it in me.

29 August 2001

Describe my driving as "unnecessarily aggressive and I will never get into a car with you again." You're a pussy.

17 August 2001

Drink the last Diet 7-Up in the community refrigerator. I bet you're the same person who sends out those crappy company emails that say "Good Work Team!" and "Our Numbers Look Great!"

14 August 2001

Forget your wallet, again, when it's your turn to pay. It's not sneaky. It's stupid.

10 August 2001

Accuse me of drugging you with my depression medication. I will tell you when I do that.

08 August 2001

Crank up the air conditioner in the office so high that every woman's chest is its own PowerPoint presentation.

07 August 2001

Call me while I'm sleeping, and after I tell you that I'm sleeping, continue to jabber like a fucking monkey.

17 July 2001

Print out something just for the specific purpose of walking behind my chair, stopping, and leaning down to smell my hair.

04 June 2001

You're cute but then you opened your mouth to speak.

01 June 2001

Invite me to a party where all the men are gay.

23 May 2001

How about some blinker action you Mitshubishi motherfucker.

Site: Dooce

URL: http://dooce.com

Broken Hearts

Choire Sicha

> Question: I have just had my heart ripped out by the love of my life. My question is: what the fuck do I do now? C.S.
>
> Answer: You have taken a very bad spill in the volleyball game of love. Let me be the lesbian physical therapist who patches you up and, with an alarming smack on the ass, sends you back in the game. You'll be spiking it again for mommy before you know it but only if we do this thing right.

Orange Vests, Black Hearts

Like a moose but a pretty moose confronted with a shotgun, you planned to spend the day just moose-ing around: grazing, dozing, copulating with a fecund moose-ette. But hunting season has other plans. There is your lover's safety-orange vest and camouflage hat, the wading boots, and, of course, the big trophy knife. (They always take a trophy.) Your plans will be revealed as stupid sylvan fantasia; and then you will see only the jagged hole, the blood, the frantic spasms of your forelegs. Your final visions are the white tails of other hooved lovers bounding fearfully away from your disaster, off into the safe forest of their loves. Everything goes black. You, alone, believe you will die.

But you will not. When you come to, you will be one very pissed-off two-ton antlered motherfucker. Drag your bloody tufty ass out of there and go home, and gore anyone who gets in your way.

Your Mommy, The Office, and Calories

Upon being dumped, go to your mommy's home. Eat whatever she has in the house. Talk or don't. Go uncomplainingly with her to the Costco for the cheap gas, driving all the way across town to save fifty cents. Do what mommy does, and always let her drive. Driving in the first four days after being dumped is highly unsafe. I speak from experience: blinded with a lethal combination of rage at and empathy for my dumper, my rental car somehow mounted a huge curb and nearly murder-ized several leather-pants-ed homosexual gentlemen on San Francisco's Market Street.

Use care: you must pretend that people are innocent, even though you currently believe otherwise.

Try to avoid your job as long as you can. (This is easiest if your dumper is also your boss. Related: you are kind of a whore.) If you go back to work too soon, you might, let's say just for a completely fictional example, burst embarrassingly into tears in San Francisco's Armani Cafe while having an otherwise pleasant if overpriced lunch with a business associate.

One final word of caution: you will either lose or gain 10 pounds in the next two weeks. For once, think about what you put in your mouth, particularly if you were dumped when your girlfriend found you going down on her brother.

Rage, the Ego, and Proud Black Women

Lil' Kim's epic song-poem "Heavenly Father" is your song until your housemate confiscates the CD. Freak out and tell him your posse's going to pull up in their Hummers and Escalades and bust his faggot head open unless he gives it back. He may cry if you are cruel enough; you may cackle at him crying. This feels great! Try it!

Rage will be your single most important tool, more than Pringles, more than Parliaments. Anger means you want to live and thrive. Whatever you do, do not suppress it. After all, if you put the cork back in half-consumed bottle of Chateau Yon Figeac, will it not soon become vinegar and go bad? But if you drink it all, it magically disappears, no? Yes. Your rage is to be drunk.

Next, turn to quotations from song stylist Erykah Badu. Here are some situations in which her wisdom becomes useful:

If someone compliments you, say, "I'd like to thank the Creator for giving me this gift, and I'd like to thank all of you for being reflections of this gift." Wander off dazedly.

Before you cook a friend a meal, say, "Keep in mind that I'm an artist, and I am sensitive about my shit."

And if things get deep, and people are prying into your breakup, pull this one out:

"Most of the time, you don't even know your mamma have a gun, you know? And when she pulls it out, and shows it to you, it's something serious. And the way life is to me right now, we're at a very detrimental time."

At last, you will graduate to Mary J. Blige's "No More Drama." Just put it on repeat. Sick of it? You're healed.

Self-Pity, Despair, and Miraculous Interventions

One day in your recovery, you will be out strolling, feeling swell. You will sit down to rest, and your brain will make you think: "I hate myself. I am X years old and I have accomplished nothing. Please, may I die?"

This is important: Do not rush home and call your ex. Do not call any of your previous ex's, not even for cheap sex.

What you must do is absolutely nothing. Accept the kind invitations of your floor; lay there endlessly. And just when you think that you will finally rise from the floor and down all the Comtrex in the house in a foolish and totally faux suicide attempt, you will receive a sign. This sign will often come from a homeless person or in a dream.

In my case the sign was the first sentence in a piece of spam email. This spam began: "Dear Friend: As you read this, I don't want you to feel sorry for me, because, I believe everyone will die someday."

I freaked. The profound implications of this were: I will die! My dumper will die! The spammer will die! In fact we will all die, and I have been spending my time perpetuating my rejection! The ultimate humiliation will be delivered, our shivering bodies spread raggedly open to the heavens of whatever God may or may not care, and each of us will go out with a silent gasp in a pool of our own congealed blood with no reason or sense. So let's party down!

Controlling Substances

You have seen fire and rain. You decide that you have recovered; an hour later you're back in the bathroom, calculating a lethal dose of Mylanta. Remember that recovery isn't linear; it zigs and zags like a cracked-out basketballer. You will lose your mind a little bit. In some midnight hour you will cry out that God is punishing you. Later, you will realize that actually, you hadn't been dating God.

Undoubtedly you've decided at least once to scale Mount Everest to reach the Valley of the Dolls, in the immortal words of self-help guru Jacqueline Susann. Make careful choices in this turbulent valley. For instance, avoid Ambien: It has a little kick at the end that prevents true enjoyment of sedation. Klonopin is a definite yes. That is some good shit, take it early and often, bro. Alcohol is tried and sometimes true, but one must be careful about one's impulse control: I have a friend, yes, a "friend," who, in a moment of impairment, wrote a long weepy humiliating email to his ex. My friend is a stupid, stupid, stupid fucking bastard friend.

Do Not Think About Your Ex Whilst Masturbating

Seriously.

Freshen Up While the Lavatory Door of Your Love Life is Set to "Occupied"

Of course you must not date immediately, at least not without full disclosure. Otherwise, you will have gone to the Dark Side. You are now

A. emotionally unavailable and

B. 10 pounds thinner (if you made the right choice early on), and when you walk the streets, heads turn. Remember the faces that are attached to these heads: They belong to the sort of people who have a sixth sense for the lovesick or damaged partner. These remoras only sup on leftovers. You must not date them at any future time, as it will clearly mean that you are still love's tragedy. Do however enjoy the validation. Wear something skimpy.

This regrouping period is a great time to prepare for when you are finally able to date. Make a list of your criteria for a future lover. You can even prepare a little test for prospective dates, and put some tricky questions in there to weed out the troubled! For example:

Q. Hey, just how much is the current monthly allotment of food stamps?

Q. Does your therapist examine your emotional life while you lay on a couch or does your therapist charge more for sessions "with release"?

And of course:

Q. What is your earliest memory of your father's erect penis?

The revelatory nature of these answers will be in direct relation to the care with which you compose the questions. As this process jumpstarts your sense of humor and your self-regard, you will have that rare Greek experience. No, the other rare Greek experience: catharsis. That catharsis will birth The Plan.

The Plan

The Plan will appear when you embrace an inner vision of the civil rights cry "Segregation never, integration now!" Your recent experiences of self-loathing and self-love will be the materials from which you will design a grand vision of the future. You were absolutely right when you despaired: You are in fact X years old, and you actually haven't done anything with your life. But it's not the tragedy you perceive. This wakeup call has given you a chance; your new perspective on life compels you now to live differently.

They say that a spiritual awakening occurs when the obvious becomes obvious. "These cigarettes won't kill me," we say with every puff. "When I was a little girl I knew I'd be a jazz singer in Harlem," we think into our pillows every night. "I've always dreamed of starring in a hardcore double-penetration video," we weep in our therapist's Upper West Side office, "and I want my dreams to come true!"

This is your moment. Your dumper's shortsighted cruelty is life's gift. Now that you're free and unafraid, you must make yourself into what you always knew you would be. Whether or not you become friends with your dumper, you will come to love him or her with gratitude as you scat away smoke-free into your own fantastic, pornographic future.

Site: Choire Sicha Dot Com

URL: http://choiresicha.com

Clutching For Answers In Baghdad

Christopher Allbritton

The streets of Baghdad are prickly with pointed questions, as residents pick at my sleeve and beg me for answers I cannot give.

"Why is there no water?"

"The river is too high and will soon flood. When will the Americans do something?"

"We need electricity and security, where is it?"

"Where are the prisoners?" asked a man who gave his name as Muhammed. "It's a simple question. What is the answer?"

All of these are asked of me, as I pick my way through the crowd outside the Hotel Palestine in downtown Baghdad. Each time I am forced to give the same answer: "I don't know. I can't help you. I'm sorry."

Two photographers, Jason and Juan Carlos, and I have driven down for the day. The drive in is pleasant, with the occasional T-72 Iraqi tank parked by the road, seemingly abandoned by the crews. Once we get to the outskirts of this sprawling city, however, the tanks and other military vehicles are bombed out and destroyed.

Baghdad itself, low-slung and dusty brown, is bustling with activity. A haze of dust clings to the ground, and mixes with the auto exhaust from the thousands of vehicles on the street. Icons of Saddam are mostly lacking; I'll bet they have been removed by U.S. troops and Baghdadis. The few posters and murals that remain are largely untouched, though. Driving in, we can see the effects of the looting and the bombing damage. Buildings marked with the Ba'ath Party eight-point star show scorch marks or are partially collapsed. Much of the city seems intact, however. Even downtown, a target-rich environment, seems more or less intact. The "precision bombing" seems to have been more or less aptly named.

The occupation is not making many friends among the Iraqis, however. In marked contrast to the welcome and friendliness we always receive in the north and in Kirkuk, the looks here are guarded and even cold. We smile and wave at people in the cars next to us when the traffic grinds to a halt, but our fellow drivers look at us and don't smile back.

There seems to be a constant demonstration going on in front of the press balcony of the hotel and as I pass, one man holds up a sign that reads, "The Americans are Lyers." Another hands me a note in both Arabic and English that reads:

Letter to Conference, Baghdad.

Dear Leaders, USA and Iraq: We are Al Shaab Native Free Party. We wanted to [attend the] meeting in Iraq with the leaders USA and Iraq. Thanks, Best.

Saeed Alifaashmi

Leader, Al Shaab Party

16/4/2003

It seems an opposition movement to the yet-to-be-installed interim government is already taking root.

The Marines here have a tough job. The populace is angry at the lack of services—no phone, water, electricity or work—and the troops are getting increasingly aggressive in the face of mounting public anger. Everyone is on a hair-trigger. The Palestine is an armed fortress, ringed by concertina wire, about 150 troops and a dozen LAVs or so. The Marines push the Iraqis back—not always gently—as they press forward to tell their stories to a trooper, the press...someone who might listen.

At one point, a group of Iraqis began shouting at the Americans guarding the press entry point to the Palestine. The Marines began shoving the Iraqis back as they chanted louder and louder in Arabic. Then, the crowd sat down on the sidewalk. "No Saddam! No Saddam!" they yelled out. They were protesting the use of Iraqi police officers and demanded the Marines provide security instead of the organs of the old regime.

"We want the Americans to cooperate with us," said Muhammad Abdul-Rasul, 46, an interpreter. "We need work. Who is in charge?" He then demanded "Mr. Bush" to turn on the public services within 48 hours.

The city is awash with conspiracy theories, the preferred method of analysis in the Middle East.

Ehsan Abud denied that Iraqis were the ones responsible for the looting and instead it's the Kuwaitis coming up to take revenge for the 1990 invasion. And Arabs, not Iraqi Arabs, went into the University of Mustemsrya in Baghdad and burned all the books. And America has trained 500 Iraqis and other Arabs in the United States, parachuted them into Baghdad (nee Saddam) International and turned them loose on the city to burn and pillage.

The Marines based around the hotel declined to comment on these accusations.

The Americans are "useless" because they have been here for 10 days and they have done nothing for the city, said Abud. He said security in some neighborhoods is provided by armed volunteers guarding the streets.

There's no doubt Baghdad is wooly at night. Marines told me they "took a guy down" last night when he was attempting to break into a media truck. Iraqis tell of the pop-pop of automatic weapons fire from all directions when the sun goes down.

The Interior Ministry is also a favorite source of rumor. This was the dreaded nexus of Saddam Hussein's security state, and many people think there are underground prisons where loved ones who disappeared 20 years ago suffer still.

"Why don't they dig under the Security building?" asked Ali Abid Khafaji. "Americans are guarding it and not letting the prisoners out."

Muhammad, the man who asked about the victims of Saddam's regime, said thousands of people are waiting to hear about their relatives and friends. Where are they? They have disappeared. "We want to know where they are," he said. "You are the media. You can tell the world. Please, help us."

Site: Back in Iraq 2

URL: http://www.back-to-iraq.com/

Interview with Christopher Allbritton of Back To Iraq

After the terrorist attacks on Sept. 11, 2001 and consequently the war in Iraq, New York reporter Christopher Allbritton felt that mainstream American media wasn't telling the public the whole story, so he took matters into his own hands. He went to Iraq to interview people and see the war firsthand, instead of relying on media gatekeepers whose desire to sell newspapers outweighed their responsibility to inform. Allbritton ended up publishing his experiences on his candid blog, Back-to-Iraq.com. Consequently, his writing was not only seen by a larger public, but his audience also helped pay for him to stay in Iraq and report, by donating funds through his blog site.

Why did you feel compelled to write about your experiences online? Why do you think your coverage of the war in Iraq was needed?

I started doing it because I had a hard time getting editors interested in my stories after my first trip there in 2002. So started Back-to-Iraq.com. Pretty soon, I realized that my desire to go had a lot to do with telling the stories I was interested in, rather than what *The New York Times* and others wanted to tell me. I didn't see nearly enough of the Iraq I saw when I was first there, and thus, the fundraising. Other people apparently felt that they weren't getting the stories they wanted to read either, and in me they found an agent who would give them what they were looking for—or at least some reasonable approximation. They sent me there to find out the Truth, which is actually impossible, but I made a pretty good stab at it and got at least a little piece of it. That's about the best a journalist in a situation like war can do, regardless of who they write for.

What were some of the challenges you faced in Iraq reporting the war through such a new medium of blogging? What did you learn from the experience?

I had no backup, for one. If something happened, who was going to come bail me out? My editor? My publisher? Nope. So I had to be pretty damn careful, both physically and journalistically. It maybe caused me to focus more on the "journalism of everyday life" that I felt the blog is ideal for showing: personal, opinionated, small, and quirky. I learned that those kinds of stories can be really rich and rewarding to report and to tell.

What has the reaction been from people (both readers and other journalists) regarding your blog reporting?

Overwhelmingly positive from both the left and the right—I got a note from Leif Utne, the editor/publisher of *Utne Reader* complimenting me, and from Lucianne Goldberg, conservative hitgirl, also complimenting me. As a leftist myself, the note from Goldberg was a little interesting, to say the least.

What do you hope people learn about you from your writing?

About me? Not a lot. I don't really want to be the story. I just want to be the vehicle for the stories that people want to read. I hope they learn that I'm honest, trustworthy, loyal, brave...You know, all that Boy Scout stuff.

Why do you think blogging has become so popular in the last few years?

Ease of use, a confessional culture that permeates America. I'm not really sure. I use a blog for the same reason I use a laptop and not a portable typewriter: it's the best tool for the job I want to do.

What are you planning on doing next?

I'm raising money for a third trip to Iraq, and I think this trip will be the longest yet. Perhaps a permanent move to the region is in order. The money raised this time will be the startup fund for establishing myself as a foreign correspondent in the region.

But first I have to finish up teaching my second semester at NYU. The spring semester is over May 3, however, and by May 6 or so, I'd like to be on a plan to the region. I won't be teaching anymore after this one. I'm better facing down guerillas than students....

Con Man

Matt Hinrichs

Please say it's just a bad dream—Converse has filed Chapter 11.

Hopefully, though, this isn't the end. Classic Chuck Taylors have too much of a loyal cult following to simply go away. Here's hoping some smart shoe company will pick up production on them. In the meantime, I present my own personal history with Cons:

Black Canvas High Tops (1984): At fourteen, Chuck Taylor high tops are an icon of coolness, a ticket into the teen world of cars and nightclubs and concerts. Saved up some chore money and bought them at the local Gemco, where a salesman helped me try them on. At size 10-1/2, they were kind of big, unwittingly contributing to the geeky "high school frosh" look I had at the time.

Red Leather High Tops (1987): After seeing exotic leather Cons in a Rolling Stone fashion spread, I decided to look for them. They're $50 at the nearby "surf gear" shop, but I bite the bullet, for coolness has no price. For about five minutes I'm cool at school; one of the class jocks even compliments me on them. Abruptly stopped wearing them a few months later, after my mom makes an offhand comment that they resemble clown shoes. Still have them in storage.

Plain Canvas High Tops (1991): Purchased at the local sports emporium, these Cons became my favorite shoes, ever. More unassumingly cool than the earlier pairs, they blend in with all sorts of outfits and become my footwear of choice between '91 and '96. Replacements are hard to find, and I have to settle for inferior J. Crew knockoffs instead. Finally threw them last year, after they started falling apart.

Teal Canvas Low Tops (1995): A lucky find at Miller's Outpost in Chandler, AZ—for the bargain price of $8. They fit perfectly and receive lots of compliments from family and coworkers. Currently, my "lounging around the house" shoes. A little worn now—the "ALL STAR" rubber rectangles on the heels fell off recently. Still incredibly cool.

Site: Scrubbles

URL: http://scrubbles.net

I Don't Know About Your Blog...

Mrs. Kennedy

...but one of the reasons this blog is so bulimically narcissisical and full of stuff that is probably only interesting to myself (hence the negative numbers in my site stats) (god, I could talk to myself for hours) (oh, wait, that's why I got married) is simply because stuff happens, and when the Alzheimer's really starts to kick in I'll be able to save myself the embarrasment of repeating the alphabet over and over again (*true story, except my grandmother had the style to do it in Swedish*). Instead, I'll just point to this site, assuming I've remembered to keep up the Hostway payments, and say, Voila, Jackson, your childhood in a bucket. On July 23, 2003, while sitting in your father's truck and listening to Stevie Ray Vaughan, you, aged two, said, "I like this guy." It was also reported that you spent the earlier part of the afternoon singing for your preschool mates, who stood in rapt attention around you. I had this fantasy that you're some drama queen like Janice Joplin, come back in the body of a little boy. And why not? Can't you just see her, laughing her fat white ass off, bossing around some big black-winged afterlife bat: "Make me into a little boy, motherfucker!" It might also account for the way you've taken, in the frustrating moments when the raisins slide off your milky cereal spoon, to saying, "Oh, goddamn it!" Although really, we have the two weeks you just spent with your grandmother to thank for that.

Site: Fussy

URL: http://whatsthefuss.com

Fuctung

Neil Forrester

1995

I was stupid enough to stick my tongue in a psychopath's mouth.

I was also stupid enough to do it while being filmed.

I was unhappy.

I wrote these things.

LANGUAGE

As Wittgenstein pointed out, there is no private language. The thoughts within my head can only mean anything when I use them in my linguistic community—the same community that gave them to me—the same community of language users and their referents that define the language.

To be unable to speak immediately places you in a passive role in this community. I have the knowledge to comprehend the utterances I find around me, but am unable to respond. Gloriously impotent.

At first it seems an attractive option, to observe passively the blatherings of my neighbours and see the mechanisms of language in action. I discovered pretty quickly that most conversation is trivial and meaningless. This was a disappointment, until I realised that this ephemera binds the language together. Very rarely is there anything of import to communicate that in itself is no reason to cease communication—people enjoy talking, it is a pleasure beyond communication.

The situation changes however, once there is something of substance to say. I find myself lost in an unknown part of town, late at night—plenty of people about yet I can speak to none of them. I am beset by fear and frustration. Unable to ask for help. The true impact of being mute becomes apparent. No fun.

Even when speech begins to return I am impeded, my usual eloquence replaced by a slurping, lisping drooling patios that's unpleasant to hear and difficult to understand. The effortless grace of conversation that we take for granted seems like a million miles away. I am humoured. There's little I hate more than being humoured. Even now, weeks later I still notice my impediment, I am reassured that no one else can hear it, but I can, I know I can.

The interesting side is that so much of linguistic interpretation is a reconstructive process. Witness the difficulties encountered when trying to fashion a machine to interpret speech. The listener brings a huge amount of information to the situation; context and syntax allow the understanding of even the most impoverished speech signal. I do not wish to be the producer of an impoverished signal. I want to be able to sing and screech like I used to. One day I might, but that day is some way off.

FOOD

The scents are intoxicating. From the instant the elements are collected together, through their paths of preparation until the completion of consumption, the scents are intoxicating. Where to start, where to start...

Perhaps at the cutting of the loaf, as the speckles of crust are dispersed into the air like so many grains of pollen. The soft yielding of the bread-flesh as the serrations of the knife tear open the tiny pockets of CO_2, unleashing to the air infinitesimal yet significant puffs of greenhouse gas and the aroma of yeast. Perhaps the slavering of the butter onto the virgin surface, coating the fronds of dough with slick yellow emulsion—the bread valiantly resisting the suffocation of its areoles yet yearning for it all the same.

Or perhaps the bacon itself, each slice clinging to its neighbour, separated but together—part of the same pig-whole, killed and prepared for my gustatory pleasure. The gentle sizzle as each rasher hits the pan and begins to exude its flavoursome juices through the folds of gently searing flesh. At once the air is filled with the musky odor of the smoked meat, inflaming my nostrils and precipitating the primary digestive saliva to come to my tongue.

I watch the slices dance around the pan, jittering and popping, shrinking and transmuting—from the flaccid slavering pink pieces to the carefully crisped mouth watering morsels. I bide my time, sensing the bread stiffen behind me—I touch its un-buttered face and find it hardening at the tips of its ripped surface, bracing itself for its ultimate noble consumption.

Once cooked the bacon is immediately transferred to the buttered plinth that begins to melt, mingling itself with the grease and oozing into the porous bread. The upper slice is placed on top and the sandwich is complete.

This is the point where I pause, become giddy with expectation as I feel the warmth of the meat work its way through the bread to my fingertips. A drop of melted butter and fat slips from between the slices and trickles into my hand. Heaven! Waiting, waiting, the time must be right before the first bite...

There, I've done it. I have violated my construction with my tearing incisors, the bread crumples under my advance and the bacon fights briefly then gives in. Only the springy crust gives me any trouble, demanding a sideways shake of the head to relinquish its hold. I have my mouthful and begin my careful mastication. There is a melee of flavour. Taste is not spatially coded, but there is the element of time. A dimension that can draw out the sensations as they overlap and separate, as the combine and recombine at once confounding my expectations and reassuring me.

As I swallow the bolus (too soon, I'm sure), I feel the knot work its way down to my stomach and unfurl—yielding itself, to be broken down and finally become a part of me.

SEX

The kiss is at once personal and casual, intimate and detached. Prostitutes, we are led to believe, indulge in intercourse without the kiss, precisely for this reason. The kiss is somehow more intimate than the sexual act itself. Since my injury was inflicted by a kiss, the impairment occurs precisely over the surface of the tongue involved in the act of kissing. Indeed there remains a possibility that sensation may never return; I am effectively, divorced from the pleasures of kiss. Forced into the domain of absolute altruism. I will kiss, only for the other, no longer for myself...

It is believed that the kiss originated as a method of passing food from one individual to another—the first communication, the first intimate socialization. Now the kiss is the ultimate in communication, the pinnacle of the lovers touch, telling everything and nothing, passing love and lust directly from one to the other. Have you ever tried sex without kissing? The act is different, lessened, certain aspects negated even. It is the essential part of any sexual encounter—the prelude and the aftermath, not to mention the catalyst of the act itself. To make love without kissing is akin to masturbation, the intimacy is gone, the communication is gone—one is left with only the base signals from the genitalia and the secondary sensations of the surface of the body. One no longer makes love, nor even fucks—one simply 'has sex'—carries out the motions of reproduction like a Mormon (though without the added fission of guilt).

Even assuming that the musculature returns to normal—without sensation I can never be kissed, I can only kiss. Indulging only in secondary labial pleasures. Indeed the tongue is the most intimate and sensitive part of the body in such situations. A good kiss is infinitely more rewarding than even the greatest fellatio. The penis feels only the sensations required to gradually build from erection to orgasm. The tongue however delights in such subtleties of sensation that one could kiss a lover forever without fear of repetition.

Currently I am partially healed. I have a viable piece of flesh—an approximation of the original organ physically, but crippled as a sensory device. I cannot extend my tongue to kiss; I cannot feel the touch of another's tongue dancing on the surface of mine. I could remain this way forever.

Site: NeilForrester

URL: http://neilforrester.com

The Gameshow

Neil Forrester

1997

If "The Real World" was a soap opera this is one big gameshow. The concept is simple, get a bunch of kids the viewers are familiar with, some old, some new and get them to compete against each other—the smoking drinking Real World kids versus the tough sporty Road Rulers. The idea is that they choose challenges that take advantage of the varying abilities of the two teams. In reality physical activity makes good TV so most of it involved running around. You can guess where that left the wheezing real worlders.

SKATES

Hell, they say, is other people. Bollocks, hell is other people on rollerskates. I have no concept of Rollerderby—we don't have in England. We have other more sensible sports like badger baiting and bare-knuckle boxing. Still, I'm along for the ride, the least I can do is give it a go. There's an obviously more commercial bent to this whole show in comparison to "The Real World," most notably on the issue of corporate sponsorship. On arrival my luggage was substituted for nice new Eastpack stuff, and again here, at Rollerderby we're all sporting shiny new RollerBalls (not available in the shops, but sure as hell will be by the time the show airs).

As far as I can tell Rollerderby is a cross between WWF and Starlight Express, though the rules are considerably more arcane. Two teams go round in circles trying to beat the crap out of each other without falling over. Great opportunity to film us falling on our arses, so far so good. I must admit, I'm not much of a team player at the best of times, put me on wheels and I just spend my time keeping out of the way. The competition itself is a taste of things to come, ravenous screaming fans bussed in from the boonies, come to see the freak show live and in effect. Is it really true that the camera puts on 10 pounds? Is Montana really a bitch? Is Noah just as dreamy in real life as he is on TV? A cheap treat where every seat in the house is free and you can almost smell the 'reality' of it all. Beth takes a dive and we see real tears, real sympathy, like on TV but without the Diet Coke break.

We came as Gladiators we left as lion food. The gonzo touring freak show limps out of town gathering corporate moss as only a multi-million dollar rolling stone can. I lie on my back to sleep, this is gonna be a hell of a ride.

WHEELS

I for one was glad to be riding in that rusting tin can This is a roadtrip sponsored by one of the worlds' biggest media corporations, the least you can do is ride in style and try to forget. The ride gets named Bessie and we drive onto our first (of many) RV parks. Personally, I was a little disappointed that we weren't in a proper trailer park, like the one I've been dreaming about ever since Jerry did his expose on alien-transsexual abduction, but it's close enough, there are overweight tourists in plaid, yapping dogs in tow, besides, we need some shuteye. I'm living in a timezone, which is 8 hours ahead, so things feel a little spooky.

The road to Mammoth is a long and winding one, but by God there's some breathtaking country up there. For a man whose experience of California is limited to the freeways of LA this is a bit of an eye opener. We make it to our new home, another RV park in the mountains, in time to find that the news of our touring gameshow has preceded us, squealing teenage campers is the last thing I wanted to see after traveling for 10 hours, so it's time to get drunk and watch the sky, the truth has gotta be out there, my god it's full of stars. This trip started as "Apocalypse Now," and rapidly turned "Easy Rider," or at least that's how I hoped. In reality it's somewhat more like "Pee-Wee's Big Adventure," but fuck it, this is Ansel Adams country and I'm lost in reverie.

We get up early and pile over to June Lakes to find out about our next 'mission'—it's a bed race, something I am more familiar with. Our challenge, decorate the bed, push it down a hill—hey, no rollerskates—I'm sold. Part of the challenge is allegedly the 'creative' aspect of the decoration and costumes, so we think we're in with a chance. Initial ideas come thick and fast. My prescience for 'fly-sandwich' with Beth as a giant bug between foam bread being pursued by swatting housewives turns out to be a no go unfortunately, so we go with the mainstream option of 'The Village People.' I've been there before (but that's a different story), the bed's a hippie mobile with Gavin at the helm, and we're the usual suspects.

We retire to the RV park and inhale more booze, American beer never really does it for me, and as for the strange fluid only know to me as 'white zinf,' what the hell is that, isn't it best saved for the express purpose of removing stubborn understains? Still the girls seem to like it. Jason and I get involved in a little freeform text on the side of the vehicle, turns somewhat into a pissing contest, but our bond is made.

Dawn rises and we're ready to go. We look great, we're feeling confident, but the thick necks win again. This is becoming a habit. Still we win a prize from the locals for our sartorial elegance. The winnie breaks down and we resort to riding in the back of the mega-bus for a while.

There's a lake, there's prescription pharmaceuticals, there's a clarity in the wintery sunshine. Tomorrow we're off to the City of Angels. We're all stars now, of the dope show.

Site: NeilForrester

URL: http://neilforrester.com

Interview with Neil Forrester of NeilForrester

Imagine living with seven strangers picked to have their lives recorded, edited, and enhanced with a trendy soundtrack, only to end up on MTV. Sound familiar? Neil Forrester found himself with a sudden dose of stardom thanks to his appearance as the debonair punk singer on *The Real World: London*. Long after his season ended up on reruns, he found himself documenting his experiences from the show online.

Why did you feel compelled to write about your experiences online?

Having been rather surprised by the version of "Neil" that made it to the screen via the editing suites of Bunim-Murray Productions, I was compelled to try and flesh-out the character that was broadcast as me with a little more substance. I'd already spent some time toying with the kids on alt.tv.real-world, first anonymously, then owning up, and I found it fascinating how the medium of the Internet, for the first time really, allowed direct and unfettered communication between "celebrities" and the public.

Particularly since the show had been a "reality" program, there seems to be this belief in the viewing community that you are public property. People make wild and quite misguided assumptions about me, based on footage I've no control over. The medium of the Internet is one of the more direct tools available to rectify this problem. Obviously, it's not the same as having your own TV channel, but it has some of the same qualities.

How has your fame in reality TV affected your writing? Do you find the online community to be more intriguing than the TV community?

I'd never really exposed my writing to the world before, and I found that once you get over the trolling, most feedback from the online community is very positive. Certainly the immediacy of being able to enter into a direct dialogue with "viewers" is an interesting concept.

In terms of the writing itself, there has been so much more weirdness in my life since that TV show, that I have plenty more material to work with!

Why do you think blogging has become so popular in the last few years?

I think there's always been a strong tradition of "journaling" amongst American youth—far more than any of my peers over here in England and online blogging is an extension of that.

If you are the kind of person who likes to spend the time writing down your thoughts and experiences, it makes sense that you're quite likely to want to show it to someone else, but probably not your nearest and dearest, hence the blog becomes the perfect way of broadcasting to strangers. And, due to the immediacy of electronic communication, you can gain an extra-dimension to your navel-gazing.

Also, there appears to be an increasing distrust of officially sanctioned sources of information, the blog is by definition a subjective perspective, but if you're able to understand this, they can be an excellent source of knowledge and opinion.

What do you hope people learn about you from your writing?

I guess if people can read it and realize that what MTV chose to show was not the whole story, then I'm happy, that they walk away with a sense that I have a personality beyond the one constructed for me.

Hester Prynne

Heather B. Armstrong

This morning I woke up only to find that I had outgrown yet another piece of clothing, a pair of pants I bought three months ago that was four sizes bigger than the pants in my non-pregnant wardrobe. This leaves me with exactly four items of clothing that I can actually wear, including a pair of my husband's plaid pajama bottoms which I am embarrassed to report don't make the best impression when worn to a business lunch.

I know it's time to invest in maternity wear. I can't continue to deny the fact that my belly has transformed into such an awkward shape that the only thing that is going to fit any longer is an industrial-sized canvas drop cloth. But I've never been a big clothes shopper, and I find it supremely hard to justify buying a pair of pants that I will only be able to wear for two months when the average life span of a pair of pants in my wardrobe is longer than the series run of "Law and Order." I'd much rather spend $50 on a really good dinner at a Thai restaurant than on a sturdy, name-brand pair of pants, even though I know the pair of pants will last 700,000 times longer than a serving of massaman curry. I know it makes no sense, but food tastes better than clothing, and that's where my priorities are.

Because I have yet to purchase any maternity clothes I'm still wearing t-shirts and sweaters from The Old Life, and this annoys the more conservative members of my family to no end. I think they see my exposed pregnant belly as some sort of scarlet letter, that I'm announcing to the world in a broad stroke of flesh that I have had sex successfully. Sadly, the only thing I'm announcing to the world by wearing a t-shirt that barely covers the top of my belly is that I gained two pounds yesterday.

I'm also supposed to be setting some sort of an example to my nieces and nephews about modesty and whatnot, and baring my mid-section in public is, I suppose, evidence that I am a coke-snorting whore for hire whose evil flesh will burn at the second coming of Jesus Christ. The last thing my family should be worried about is what my clothes are saying to their children, which is, if you listen really closely, "Dressing in clothes that are too small for your body, like Aunt Heather does, makes you look COMPLETELY FUCKING RIDICULOUS." They should be much more concerned with how I plan to dispose of the bodies of their children after I sacrifice them at the alter of Satan, which has been my master plan ever since I left the church and started reading Noam Chomsky.

I will eventually give in and start wearing those atrocious pup tents they try to pass off as clothing, the shirts that flare with a full 15 foot circumference at the waist. And if I have to I'll even get a pair of elastic-bellied denim trousers that do nothing but make pregnant women look like cheap concubines in Humpty Dumpty's harem. I'll buy into it all, for crying out loud, but in the meantime my family is going to have to get over my bare belly and all the sinful, successful sex that got it here in the first place. I should point out that since Jon and I are married, our sinful, successful sex is state-sanctioned, which in Utah means approved by God. So my bare belly is, for all intents and purposes, a righteous, God-fearing belly with a place reserved in heaven for itself and all its polygamist wives.

Site: Dooce
URL: http://dooce.com

My Cred Is Intact

Matthew Baldwin

A coworker walked by my office and overheard the mp3 I was listening to. "Oh my God!" she exclaimed. "Are you listing to The Backstreet Boys?!!"

"No, of course not!" I replied guiltily. "Like I'd listen to The Backstreet Boys! Yeah, right! Hah hah! Hah! No, this is a parody of The Backstreet Boys called 'E-Bay'." By Weird Al Yankovic."

Whew—that was close! Thank goodness I was able to explain to her that I was listening to Weird Al—otherwise she might have thought I was a dork.

Site: Defective Yeti

URL: http://www.defectiveyeti.com

Interview with Matthew Baldwin of Defective Yeti

Computer programmer and writer Matthew Baldwin didn't realize when he began writing down his daily meanderings on his blog DefectiveYeti.com how many people would read it. Writing about everything from a childhood experience meeting Darth Vader to America's lack of math skills, Baldwin grabs bits and pieces of pop culture references and blends them with unique insight and humor.

What's the name of your blog? Why is it named that?

The phrase "defective yeti" was just a bizarre combination of words that tumbled out of my mouth one day in the middle of a conversation. It popped into my head as something memorable and fun to say when I started my blog a few weeks later, so I stuck it in as a placeholder for an actual title. Alas, my inherent slackerness ensures that anything done as a stopgap measure eventually becomes the standard, so my blog has been named "Defective Yeti" ever since.

Why did you feel compelled to write about your experiences online?

I'd tried to keep pen-and-paper journals in the past, but always lacked the discipline to keep at it for any appreciable length of time. Part of the problem was the aforementioned slackerness, but there was also a component of ego: the thought that no one (myself included) would ever read what I was writing gave me little incentive to continue.

Then, while in the Peace Corps, I figured out how to trick myself into writing. I kept journals in 48-page notebooks and sent them home to my girlfriend whenever I filled one up. Knowing that I had a reader who expected output from me on a semi-regular basis gave me the motivation to write nearly every day.

After returning to the States and marrying the girlfriend, I thought my motivation for writing was permanently 86'd. But it had just gone into hibernation for a few years, awaiting the advent of blogging. In January 2002 I started Defective Yeti, and resumed my program of writing several times a week. As with the letters from Bolivia, the assumption of a hypothetical reader keeps me going—it's just that, now, all the world is my girlfriend.

Why do you think blogging has become so popular in the last few years?

I always find it curious when the media hails blogs as some crazy, unforeseen fad, instead of a logical extension of the World Wide Web.

People seem to have forgotten that, way back in 1998, the promise of the Internet was that everyone would have a voice in the global community. No longer would you have to write a letters to your local newspaper or sign up for time at the public access TV station; now you could slap together a home page and put it out there for the whole world to admire.

And so people began hacking out HTML code, building shrines to their families or their cats or, regrettably, Kid Rock. They weren't anywhere near as sophisticated as today's websites, but, in spirit, they weren't that dissimilar from blogs as we now know them.

Then the Dot Com Boom came along and, as with so many other forms of media, people got bamboozled into thinking that the real function of the Internet was to make a few people a whole bunch of money. One minute we were talking about how great it was that Grandma Grummly could publish her pie recipes online; the next all anyone could talk about was how potbelliedpigsonline.com had 74 million in venture capital and no business plan.

Well, the boom went bust, but Grandma Grummly is still putting those pie recipes online. But now, because she's using Livejournal to publish her page, she's suddenly part of the "Blogging Phenomenon."

Yes, tools like Blogger or Moveable Type make online publishing more accessible; yes, more people than ever are out there making sites. But I still think it's silly to refer to blogging as a Revolution. The Internet was the Revolution; Blogging is just fulfilling the promise.

For me, one of greatest joys in the world is being told an amusing anecdote by a master storyteller. I'm lucky to have some friends who can recount the most mundane experience, a trip to the dentist, say, in a way that will give you a stitch from laughing. There's something about the way they tell them that says, "Listen; this story may not be 100% true—some stuff has been embellished, and I've polished up the dialogue a bit—but the essence is real, and that's good enough."

It's no surprise, then, that my favorite weblogs are of the storytelling variety: blogs devoted to stories that have been "improved" a bit but come across as essentially true. In fact, I consider a writer who can integrate creative flourishes into a story to be more sincere than someone who just recites the facts, because the former tells you something about himself while he spins his yarn. And I think this aspect of weblogging—that people don't just make a website, they personalize it—accounts for much of the current and continued popularity of blogs.

Celebrity Sightings From Antiquity

Mrs. Kennedy

Who: JOHN MALKOVICH

Where: The bag check counter at Shakespeare & Co. on lower Broadway in NYC.

When: After Dangerous Liaisons but before Sheltering Sky.

What'd he do? Surrendered a flaccid suede backpack to me. I gave him a claim check.

What was the vibe? Angst-ridden. I think he was trying to be Unnoticeable Guy, and the fact that I recognized him and was freaking out six different ways on the inside was clearly visible through my frozen, bunny-in-the-headlights expression.

Coworkers' reaction: Only the theater students were impressed.

Who: MICHELLE PFEIFFER

Where: Same place.

When: After Baker Boys but before Batman.

What'd she do? Asked for a copy of Silence of the Lambs during that hopeless period where the hardcover is out of stock and the paperback isn't in print yet, which meant I had to tell her that God himself couldn't get a copy. She asked me to call around anyway. I handed her off to Andy, who clearly was dying to get involved in a lost cause with her.

What was the vibe? Casual. She showed me where she'd lost a snap on her leather jacket, then said she was on her way to the airport.

Coworkers' reaction: Later, in the stock room, Andy asked everyone if her lipstick color didn't remind us of a used tampon.

Who: MEL GIBSON

Where: The lobby below the marketing offices at Paramount.

When: After Jack and I had made our ill-fated move to L.A. but before he asked me to marry him.

What'd he do? He did a double take and then stared as I was going into the elevator.

What was the vibe? Naah, he's ~~too short old Catholic Australian~~ married.

Coworkers' reaction: I got trumped by a sighting of two producers in a limo picking up a prostitute outside of Todd AO and then bringing her back to the exact same spot three minutes later.

Site: Fussy

URL: http://whatsthefuss.com

My Beautiful Life? Not Exactly.

Allison Lowe

Into our home-life has recently bounded the smelly, hair-covered, dog-breathed, chewing machine known as Murphy. Despite his unquestionable adorableness, it has not been easy.

This is not one of those dogs that sits quietly at his master's feet, staring upward, his eyes filled with loyalty, just waiting to fulfill some emotional need with a warm nuzzle or lick to the hand.

No. Murphy leaps boisterously above his master's head, lunging wildly, his eyes filled with crazed daring, just waiting to "playfully" chew off the nearest appendage before he falls into a comatose sleep after which he will wake up and eat the couch, with a side of your best shoes, please.

To say that he has a personality of his own—hell, to say he has an agenda of his own, would be putting it rather mildly.

We tried crate training, highly recommended by dog trainers to get your new pet accustomed to your home and teach him who's boss in a harmless, helpful training exercise.

The dog can get out of the crate. I don't mean he can somehow open the door and get out. He Houdinies himself out by sliding out the bottom tray, wedging himself between the bars, and lifting the thing over his head. Let me tell you something, coming home to find your dog casually reclining on your bed, chewing through a magazine, while his crate, which you locked him in hours before, sits pristinely in the corner with the door still closed, is enough to make you very afraid.

Murphy has climbed the corporate ladder of our little community and is now the big boss of the house. For weeks, we have been running around our apartment, trying everything under the sun to get him to shut up, calm down, quit scratching, stop biting and "for God's sake, try to keep that animal from flying at my head."

We are like the parents of quadruplets, with all the action that goes on. Working to satisfy his desires so that he will not destroy our property or get us evicted has become our main concern. I swear, if he wasn't so cute, he would have "come up missing" a while ago. On the rare occasion that he does act right and not like he has rabies, he is the sweetest, most precious little dog in the world.

At moments like those, I will turn to the CHRIS and say, "I love this dog."

He will invariably answer, "You mean the dog you were choking a minute ago?"

The three of us have a complicated relationship.

I haven't watched a full hour of television, read more than two paragraphs of a book or magazine, or enjoyed much in the way of the pleasures of the pre-marital bed since he came to live with us. Is this what parenthood is like? Or is parenthood easier?

In the last week, the CHRIS and I have had secret meetings to strategize how the law will be laid down in the future. First, we had to agree on a few obvious points:

1. If any paper product exists in Murph-snatching range, that paper product becomes the property of the dog.

2. The dog does not speak English. "NO!" means nothing to him. We might as well be shouting "EAT IT!" or "BARK SOME MORE!"

3. After attempting several rescue missions of various household items, including the toilet brush, concessions were in order and compromises necessary to bring satisfaction, and thus peace, to all parties.

Working within these parameters, we made the following adjustments, which have been moderately successful.

1. All extraneous paper has been removed from the surfaces of the apartment. All trash receptacles have been placed out of reach of the dog, who though less than one foot high, can jump like Michael Jordan.

2. A rolled-up newspaper and a spray-bottle have been employed for self-defense against the dog's constant household- and owner-abuse.

3. We just went ahead and bought Murphy his own toilet brush.

Clearly, you now see before you the words of a woman who has reached the limit of her patience. I sleep every night with a spray bottle in one hand, a newspaper in the other, and my elbow curled around a plastic toilet brush. I believe this would fall under the heading "no way to live." We get about three minutes of peace before Murphy leaps into the room, flings himself on the bed and finds a comfy spot ON MY PILLOW which puts him in prime position for chewing my hair.

At first, we ignore his rude behavior, whispering to each other "If he thinks we're dead, he'll fall asleep!" Most of the time, however, he doesn't buy it, and begins his nightly ritual of gnawing on our foreheads before prancing to the middle of the bed to try to dig his way into the mattress. This causes Chris and I both to jump up, spritzing the water, whapping the newspaper, yelling and waving the toilet brush like mad, all to be met with Murphy's blinking, momentary astonishment before he joins in the fun by barking out the Hallelujah Chorus at 100 decibels.

The barking gets him a spritz in the face, which works pretty well, until the shock that I would dare defy him wears off and he starts again. Last night, I gave him such an evil look while wielding the water bottle his way, he reflected that perhaps it was time to take it easy, curled up and promptly fell into a blissful slumber, complete with snoring.

All of this has made it necessary for us to turn to a professional for help. Murphy starts training classes at the end of this month. I just hope he doesn't get kicked out of school.

I wish we could call the crazy Pet Psychic for him, but I am pretty sure he's a tough nut to crack when it comes to all that magical mystery stuff...unless, of course, she uses a toilet brush as a wand.

The CHRIS had this to add:

We have high hopes for the training process. Unfortunately, they are the same kind of high hopes Nurse Ratchett had for Jack Nicholson after they gave him a lobotomy in *One Flew Over the Cuckoo's Nest.*

It may be no way to live for the dog, but explaining to the cashier at the grocery store why I have a three inch scar over my right eye and am purchasing the sixth toilet brush in as many weeks isn't any way to live, either.

Site: Hate Your Daddy

URL: http://hateyourdaddy.com

Drew's Blog

Mike Monteiro

Drew's blog was full of interesting information.

For example; you could keep track of recent events in Drew's life and get short reviews of books that Drew had recently read as well as get an up-to-the minute feed of whatever music Drew was listening to. For a while, he'd posted a map locating his whereabouts on the planet, but after he was laid off from his product manager's job at a major Internet portal Drew found himself spending a lot of time in his apartment, so he'd discontinued the map.

His review of the latest Postal Service album was both touching and insightful, and contained a link through which you could purchase the album from a major online retailer while giving him a small share of the profit.

Lately, he'd developed a fondness for sitting on the couch watching nature documentaries and would post interesting tidbits which he figured other people would find amusing. For example; on September seventh Drew's post concerned the honey badger, believed by many naturalists to be the meanest animal in all of Africa. The honey badger's standard method of attack was different than most predators in that it went not for the throat, but for the genitals. Drew peppered this post with several cleverly obfuscated but pointed references to past coworkers.

When Drew's laundry was swiped from a dryer last summer he blogged his indignation immediately. And although he lost some good t-shirts, including his favorite "troublemaker" t-shirt, he made two new friends that day. Both Andrew and Melissa e-mailed him to express their solidarity as fellow laundry victims.

Drew's blog was touching lives.

Site: Biggerhand

URL: http://biggerhand.com

It's All In The Packaging

Matt Hinrichs

Being the frivolous person that I am is tough. Others worry about the President's speech on Cuba, or the continuing strife and unease in the Middle East, I obsess over...snack food packaging. Specifically, Pringles and Doritos—both of which have unveiled redesigned looks lately. The changes are so new they even still have examples of the old looks on their websites.

Doritos is an interesting case. I have nostalgic feelings for their '70–'80s logo—elegant serif type on alternating orange and yellow blocks that made for a kind of sprightly, Jetsons-esque look. A subsequent redesign in the '90s kept the typography, but introduced bold paint swashes and names (Nacho Cheese became Nacho Cheesier), resulting in a more "edgy" and "extreme" image. The newest redesign uses a logo made with the very '80s Crillee Italic font, the same typeface seen on repeats of "Star Trek: The Next Generation." Needless to say, it conjures up images of Capt. Picard and Data sharing a bag of Nacho Cheesier on the Bridge.

Pringles was born in the '70s; the stiff collared, mustachioed man in their logo reflects that decade's brief infatuation with early 1900s whimsy. Apparently his name is "Mr. P"—which makes me want to start a petition that forbids all companies from applying humiliating nicknames to their beloved icons. Anyway, Mr. P has gotten a makeover. What used to be simple and symmetrical is now all skewered and cartoony. Instead of resembling a pinstriped dandy from the corner barbershop quartet, he now looks like your embarrassing drunk uncle at the family Christmas party. This is an improvement?

I guess I'm just disappointed that whenever a corporate logo reaches a level of hip, retro funkiness, they change it. Burger King did this a couple of years ago. Now everything they put out looks cranked out by some kid going crazy with Photoshop's Halftone Pattern filter. When will they ever learn?

Site: Scrubbles

URL: http://scrubbles.net

Interview with Matt Hinrichs of Scrubbles

Freelance designer and illustrator Matt Hinrichs adds more than just the usual daily banter similar in many blogs. He includes an appreciation of graphic design that seems vacant in the blogging community. To him, Scrubbles.net is a labor of love. And it shows. When he's not blogging away, he's promoting his book *Mama Cat*, a children's book about dealing with a family pet's death.

Why did you feel compelled to write about your experiences online?

In the spring of 2000, I was getting bored with writing music reviews on the side of my job at the paper. So I started the weblog as a creative outlet just to write whatever was on my mind and share any cool sites I came across. It was more or less a whim of a project that has had surprising longevity.

Why do you think blogging has become so popular in the last few years?

More than anything, the rising popularity of weblogs is the result of a compromised media landscape. The less meaningful content we get from our news and entertainment outlets, the more need there is for opinionated, quirky content made by individuals. Weblogs fill that gap.

It's been very interesting how weblogs have grown since I started. Back then, they seemed very insular and clique-ish. Those qualities are still around, but now there are so many weblogs that each one is a little universe in itself. It's fascinating. For the future, I'd like to see journalists from more established media outlets try their hand at weblogs—like the ones at MSNBC.com and Artsjournal.com. Also, I'd like to see a broader range of people doing weblogs on narrower topics. Like, why isn't there a vintage dinnerware collecting weblog by now?

Close

Matthew Baldwin

I was in an elevator with a half a dozen others. As the doors started to close, a woman sprinted towards us yelling "wait!" I was closest to the control panel, so I started jabbing the "Open Door" button. But to no avail: the doors slid shut unabated. Our last glimpse of the woman was of her running, reaching out, desperately trying to catch the edge of the door. I turned to the other people in the car and flashed them a "well, I tried!" smile.

As we started moving, I glanced down and noticed that I had been pressing the "Close Door" button by mistake. A moment later it occurred to me that everyone in the elevator had watched me frantically press the "Close Door" button as the woman had tried to board, and then grin about her failure to make it in time.

This is why I now take the stairs.

Site: Defective Yeti

URL: http://www.defectiveyeti.com

A Chair! A Chair! My Kingdom For A Chair!

Heather Havrilesky

An incredibly comfortable chair. One that looks nice. I just want to be able to sit and type without having to use any muscle in my body except my fingers and maybe my brain muscle.

What? The brain is not a muscle? Maybe your brain isn't a muscle, you mental weakling, but mine is. My brain muscle says that your flabby brain doesn't know what the hell it's talking about.

Seeing as how my brain muscle is very large, I'd prefer not to have to hold up my head; I would like my head propped up gently by some soft part of the chair. Is that so wrong? Maybe there could be a downy soft head cushion on the chair. But the back part has to be ergonomic, but ergonomic in that way where you can sort of slouch without ruining your back. I write my best stuff when my spine is curved in a C shape. I'm the slouching genius, damn it, and I want a Slouching Genius Chair!

I'd also like a little desky thing where I can put a beverage. Maybe a desky thing with a cup holder. Better yet, I'd like one of those hats you can put beverages in. Then I can sip them through a straw whenever I feel thirsty, but there'll be no threat of my spilling said beverage on my keyboard—a very real threat indeed, when you own a flimsy Titanium G4 and the motherfucking motherboard is just under the keyboard, millimeters away from your grubby fingers. But the real point is, I want to remain in the slouching position—I don't want to have to fucking sit up to reach for my stupid drink. I only want to have to move my fingers and my mouth, nothing else. Don't fucking go down that path, you disgusting perverted monkeys.

I want a peddle that changes the channels on my TV. Maybe one that's connected to my TiVo, so I can fast forward through the dull parts and still type like the wind. I want a robot who'll answer my phone, and also call publicists and make nicey nice with them, and become their friends and take them out to drinks and learn all of the complicated relationships between them, and then exploit those relationships to get advance tapes and interviews with key figures from the entertainment universe. I'm not malevolent enough to do this dirty work; I prefer to spend my time here, in my lair, barely moving at all.

I have a stupid office chair, but the point is, I don't want to have to sit upright at a desk. Sitting upright at a desk makes me feel like I'm working or something. I prefer for my posture to give the illusion of slacking around the house without a care in the world. Otherwise I feel like I'm working, like I have a job or something. I must trick myself, I must never, ever catch wind of the fact that I have a job with responsibilities and obligations. Otherwise, the brain muscle feels weak and won't wrinkle upon demand. If the brain muscle thinks its being forced to exert itself for pay, it sighs deeply and says, "I can't think of anything. I'm tired. I need chocolate to think."

Here are some of the seating arrangements I've tried...

To All The Chairs I've Loved Before

1. crappy expensive ergonomic office chair (not an Aeron chair or anything, I'm not the Prince of Siam): neck and shoulders ache after a few hours, and big knots form in back; boyfriend feels knots and says, "You're so tense! It's ridiculous how tense you are!" with disgust in his voice, and then you feel guilty for being so fucking tense unlike Mr. Fucking Relaxy over here

2. stuffed, shapeless couch: like the extended legs, but propping head up just enough to see the screen leads to backaches, impromptu naps, growing lack of self-respect

3. one of those cheap Ikea chairs, you know, with the wood frames and interchangeable cushions that are so comfy in the store?: looks crappy in apartment, head cushion makes neck hurt, wooden arms chafe elbows, and guests avoid it like the plague, for fear of having someone snap a picture of them seated in such awfully uncool furniture

4. futon with special pillow and less special pillow cushioning back and propping up big head: best configuration yet, but probably not the healthiest set-up, plus, futon is ugly as sin, must sit up with great effort to reach beverages, legs get cramped when folded under body, and, on moving day, futon frame transforms into torture device that's impossible to move without breaking several fingers. You know this, so you busy yourself with some boxes while your innocent friends approach futon, unawares, as you avert your eyes guiltily. Merely considering the possibility of moving to a new place brings on a growing sense of dread over unleashing this demon on the world once more, even if the victims are just those

guys who hang out at the Home Depot looking for work, those guys who you have trouble hiring to help you move anyway because you feel so bad that anyone is forced to hang out at the Home Depot looking for work, and even though you'd be giving them work, which would be better than not giving them work, it makes you feel terribly ill to consider how your pathetic brain muscle winces and whines at the threat of cushy, white collar labor which barely requires you to lift your head when you could be an illegal immigrant having your fingers—fingers that you depend on, fingers that do hard labor so you can feed your family—snapped in half by some spoiled chick's demonic futon. Plus, this isn't even your futon, it's your exboyfriend's, the one who's been married for about a year now, amazingly enough, considering you were still going out with him about a year and a half ago. He called recently which means he might just ask for his futon back, which, pathetically enough, you'd prefer that he not do, considering it's the only seating arrangement that's worked out for you, albeit with some help from your special pillow and that other pillow you don't think about too much because it doesn't have its own blog. Still, you have a feeling he doesn't want his crappy futon back, and if he ever reads this he'll pity you and mull over all of your weaknesses for the umpteenth time, which is OK since you occasionally mull over his weaknesses, since that was sort of a little hobby you two shared for a while and old habits die hard.

5. filthy armchair at local coffee place: something about the geeky hipster clientele who, for example, laugh outloud while they're reading a book, not just outloud but loudly in a way that says, "Look at me, enjoying my book so very much!" or the way they bring their printers to the place and plug them in and print shit out with them, something about these increasingly young and sometimes vaguely irritating humans keeps your mind off your aching back, at least until you walk out the door and down the block with your heavy computer and your big bag and then your back hurts like crazy, plus you start to sweat and when you get home, you feel like you really do deserve some chocolate.

Site: Rabbit Blog

URL: http://rabbitblog.com

Cat Magnet

Mrs. Kennedy

This morning Jack[5] did this thing where he held his hand out, palm down, about a foot over the bed and Kitty would come put her head under it like he was going to pet her, but he wouldn't, he'd keep his hand above her head and then move it away and she'd stretch her neck out and walk around the bed to follow his hand wherever he moved it. This went on for about two minutes and finally Jack said, delightedly, "I have a cat magnet in my hand!"

I left a note in my daily planner that says, "All my bras are crap but I get laid anyway."

On Sunday our New York Times sat out on the lawn in its half-open blue plastic wrapper soaking up a lot of dew, so I called the bastards up and instead of asking them to deliver another paper I said I wanted the $5 unreadable wet paper credit. Then I went into the kitchen and dried the paper out in the oven section by section. And Jack watched all this (while reading the L.A. Times, which I hate and cannot read except for the Hot Property column and the comics) and said, "That is exactly what your dad would do." Because my dad will go to great lengths to save a buck, and I grew up eating a lot of discount dinners, but I also went to a good college without asking for a dime in student loans because my parents had saved up and paid my tuition in cash, so I can't really say that much against the

5. Jack is her husband.

habit, except for maybe that if you have a lifelong habit of deferring all your pleasures until later you may find that later never comes and you're so used to making do that you never learn the difference between the thing in itself is fantastic and it's great because we got it 30% off. However, when it comes to reading a wrinkly five-dollar paper for free on Sunday morning, I got no problem.

Site: Fussy

URL: http://whatsthefuss.com

Worthless Public Defenders

Greg Apt

Worthless Public Defenders

Such a concept certainly exists, and it appears to exist to a large extent in Nevada. I won't pretend to know everything about the public defender's offices in Las Vegas, but on the face of it, something is wrong.

It took me over 7 years before I was allowed to handle cases where the defendant was eligible for death, and if I actually got a case where death was a good possibility, I would have a co-counsel, probably one with death penalty experience. Apparently, in Las Vegas, if you fail a lie detector test (i.e.,—the office thinks you are guilty), they assign you a brand new lawyer, reserving their "good lawyers" for "innocent" clients. CNN has a story about this, and the subsequent lawsuit where an exonerated death row inmate has sued the office for assigning a brand new lawyer on his death penalty case because they felt he was guilty.

I say sue, and get yourself a huge amount of money.

It should not matter to a lawyer whether a person is innocent or not. Of course it does, in reality, but such a consideration should not affect the manner of your reprsentation of a client. I will not put my head in the sand and pretend that individuals are not emotionally affected by this realization, but in Las Vegas, the office apparently has a policy of disciminating between cases in this manner.

Where I work, our best lawyers have worked on cases where the defendant was absolutely guilty, in fact, I would venture a guess that if you asked most lawyers (true believers, or those who think everyone is innocent, aside), they will probably admit that they have never had a murder where they absolutely believed that the defendant was innocent. Not guilty, maybe, but absolutely innocent? I have some news for you, it doesn't happen too often. On a death penalty case? Even less frequently. There may not be strong evidence of a person's guilt, there may be justification for the killing, but the absolute wrong person? It just doesn't happen that often. If I had to wait for one of those cases before I started working hard, I would not have anything to do.

Sometimes, your best effort is getting a dead bang guilty murderer life in prison instead of death, or a non-life sentence, or a verdict of guilty to a lesser offense. Fighting a case does not mean your only hope is to have a client walk out of the front door at the end of the proceeding. The Las Vegas PDs office, if the story is to be believed, will only work hard on those few cases.

Such an office, if true, should be disbanded and put back together in a responsible manner, where all defendants have true representation by dedicated lawyers. I certainly hope the allegations are false, because if they are true, they give public defenders everywhere a black eye.

Site: Public Defender Dude

URL: http://publicdefenderdude.blogspot.com/

Interview with Greg Apt of Public Defender Dude

Watching court drama on TV, do you ever wonder what the hell a Public Defender does? Why does a lawyer choose to defend supposed criminals for a living? Asked one too many times, "So is your client innocent or does it matter?" lawyer Greg Apt decided to discuss his career on his blog, Public Defender Dude. Writing about everything from corrupt lawyers to necessary politics, his blog isn't just interesting reading, it's almost essential to anyone who wants a better grasp of the judicial system from someone who knows.

Why did you feel compelled to write about your experiences as a Public Defender in a blog?

I have always felt that Public Defenders were much maligned and little understood. There is now plenty written about criminal defense lawyers (i.e., *The Practice*), but still, Public Defenders are always considered to be the lowest of the low. I knew that was false, I figured I could give people a real world understanding of what great lawyers many of us really are, at least here in California. (I hear enough stories that suggest public defenders in other jurisdictions really can be dumping grounds for otherwise poor lawyers. I don't know how true that is, but I know here in California it is almost universally untrue.)

What has the reaction been from people regarding your blog?

I have not told anyone that I know about the blog, including my wife. I like the anonymity. I figure if my name gets out here, whatever; I've hit the big time, I can handle it. I didn't want to go trumpeting myself to people that I knew and be seen as pompous or a know it all.

The reaction from readers has been terrific. A couple of people have pooh-poohed my site, but most people have seemed to like it. That being said, it seems like I get a sort of self-selecting group of people—people inclined to agree from the start, and I really wish that wasn't the case. However, I've never really done much to advertise the site, people have just sort of run across it. When I got a site-meter that showed I had over a thousand hits in a month or two, I was floored. Now, I know what "hits" means, and it may not mean much. But, when discussion is generated on the feedback area, I love it, negative or positive.

I almost wish for more negative feedback, to get discussion going, and to generate a little controversy. However, there has been mostly nice feedback, so very little controversy. But, hey, I'm a Public Defender—I thrive on controversy!

What do you get asked most about regarding your job as a Public Defender?

People ask me the question you'd most expect: What do you do when you know a client is guilty, are you still trying to get him off, does it matter to you, etc. These seemingly confusing issues (to any non-Public Defender) are actually very easy, and are some of the reasons I created this blog.

What do you hope people learn about you from your writing?

I want people to understand the important place in society for criminal defense lawyers in general, and Public Defenders in specific. I want them to understand that people aren't Public Defenders because they couldn't get a job begging on the street, so they had to settle for this. I want people to realize that we have an exalted position, that we are honorable and skilled lawyers. I don't want people to just assume that because someone is represented by a Public Defender, they're in deeper trouble than they would be if they had some high-priced private lawyer.

Do you read other people's online journals? If so, who? If not, why?

I love reading other journals. This is what got me started. I read a lot of political ones, but I also read some personal ones where seemingly ordinary (I say "seemingly" advisedly, many are extraordinary) people write about very meaningful events in their lives, and the lives of those around us. I've also gained insight into people who may live 5 miles from me and still live a completely different life from my own.

Why do you think blogging has become so popular in the last few years?

I heard said that terrorism was the privatization of war, meaning, individuals could conduct war against large countries. I'm not comparing blogging to terrorism, but blogging is the privatization of journalism and publishing. This allows regular people to be heard worldwide. The only downside is that so many people do it so it is easy to be drowned out. However, a simple perusal of random blogs shows you how many people have very interesting things to say and recount. It is so simple to do, and you can really affect huge amount of random people by doing so.

What Up, Boss

Matthew Baldwin

While at work I frequent a website where users post interesting pictures and audio clips they have found. Today a guy who works at an ad agency posted an mp3 along with this comment: "I found this audio at the start of one of our spare tapes. No explanation, no reason it should be there. Seems to be a kid's tv program host teaching kids slang. It's overmodulated and pretty strange." I was rockin' out to Kosheen at the moment, but was sufficiently intrigued to stop my CD and click the link. A little box popped up to tell me that the mp3 was downloading and would autolaunch in winamp after a minute or so.

A few moments later by boss strolled into my office. I swiveled around in my chair to face him, turning my back to my computer. "Hey Matthew," he said sitting down,"How are you doing for time? Would you be interested in working on a new project?"

A loud voice from behind me suddenly bellowed "Awwwwwwwwwww yeah! Fo shizzle!"

Site: Defective Yeti

URL: http://www.defectiveyeti.com

Neighbor

Heather B. Armstrong

Someone downstairs is taking a shower, right now. I know they know that I shower at the same time every morning, this time, this moment right now, and I can't understand why they would choose to shower when they know that I'm usually showering right this instant.

I bet it's the girl who lives directly beneath me, in Apt #1. I think her name is Dana. Sometimes I steal her Pottery Barn catalogs on my way out to work in the morning, but I always return them to the pile of discarded junk mail in the evening so that she never knows it was gone. That way everyone wins.

She doesn't seem like the Pottery Barn type, really. I saw her once as she was taking her laundry out of the dryer. She's got long black hair, ratted and dry, and it hangs down over her shoulders like a fern that hasn't been watered in weeks. She uses Tide, with bleach, and washes her lights and darks together. Anyone who shops at Pottery Barn knows that you shouldn't co-mingle the lights and darks.

Dana drives a black Jeep Wrangler, to match her hair I've often wondered. It's a hard top, fairly well maintained with a green sticker on the bumper that says, "END RACISM." She once left a handwritten note on the windshield of my car asking me to park closer to the wall because she was having trouble fitting the Jeep in the driveway. It said something like, "It would help others" if I did this or that or whatever, I forget, but I think she meant it would just help her. That's all she cared about.

Right now she is taking a shower when she knows that I should be showering. Everyone in the building knows that two people can't possibly shower at the same time; there just isn't enough hot water. It would help me if she wouldn't shower when I'm supposed to be showering. I'm going to write a note.

Sometimes she listens to Pearl Jam in the middle of the day on the weekends. I've never complained to the landlord because, well, I'm better than that. More importantly, I would never shower at a time when she usually showers. I may, however, key her Jeep.

Site: Dooce

URL: http://dooce.com

Hey! Parking Lot Blowjob Man!

Mrs. Kennedy

I rarely think about posting something while I'm experiencing it, but...

Hey! Parking Lot Blowjob Man! Dude, I saw you cruising through Macy's at lunchtime the other day. One look at those shoes and I knew it was you. What are you, Roumanian or something? Nothing against Roumanians, my sister-in-law married (and divorced) a Roumanian and he was one charming motherfucker, even as they drove through Polish police checkpoints, at night, in the winter, in some crap Roumanian car, to bring his mother a Christmas present of several jugs of cooking oil. But whatever about that—who's your partner there with the severely eighties bleached mushroom hair and the bright yellow vest-and-slacks outfit? You guys must be the toast of Bucharest. No wonder homeless girls fling themselves at you. Good luck on that threesome with the retarded girl who sweeps up at Salvation Army that you're trying to set up for later. You guys rock.

Site: Fussy

URL: http://whatsthefuss.com

Letter From New York City's President

Choire Sicha

Dear Choire,

I've had a few questions about your city for some time now. Seeing as how you are the President of New York, perhaps you can provide me some insight.

I loved the city. Always exciting, always something to do. I stayed in a little flophouse-turned-hostel on the Bowery. Before my first day had passed, I decided that I'd have to live in New York at some point. However.

The few classified ads in New York for computer programmers read, "Programmer wanted. 15 years experience with every technology you've ever heard of, plus master's degree in Computer Science required. 80 hours a week minimum. Starting pay: $25,000/year." Further compounding my amazement was the realization that the cheapest fifth floor studio walkup in Manhattan starts at $1000 a month. *Starts* at $1000 a month.

From these factors, I concluded that either:

A Nobody who actually lives in Manhattan actually works; they all inherited gargantuan estates from rich industrialist grandparents and live off the interest. The jobs I see advertised in Manhattan are filled by people who commute from Hoboken, or,

B The help wanted ads in the newspapers are merely a deterrent to casual outsiders seeking to infiltrate the city. The real jobs are filled by word of mouth, and if I lived there for a month I could meet the right people and get a $100,000 a year computer job through the social network.

Could you provide any insights as to how this process works?

Another thing that amazed me is the incredible pomposity of the art crowd. As you wrote in your Chelsea piece in the Morning News, virtually unknown artists sell art consisting of pieces of plywood with putty filling the knot-holes on the scale of $40,000 a piece. How, exactly, does one do this? I can paint; I can draw. I saw paintings that were just a canvas entirely painted the same shade of day-glo orange selling for thousands of dollars. Someone just took a large brush and some day-glo paint, covered a canvas with one color, and attached a price tag. Is it just a matter of becoming friends with the right gallery owners?

I look forward to any mystical insights you may be able to offer.

Sincerely,

Paul

Dear Paul,

Since the legal decision which finally rightly resulted in me being "elected" New York City's President earlier this year, my office has received many a letter of complaint and confusion about my delicious city. In general, I don't answer these. I could care. I'm far too busy cleaning body parts off the skids of Bloomberg's helicopter, doing Guggenheim Museum benefit seating charts since half their staff has been laid off, and settling disputes in the Observer's "newsroom" regarding above-the-fold placements (Martha is out, the new caustic anti-imperialist pseudo-earnestness is in). My job here really is to be the magical helper that makes everything better and funner, and believe me, it's fucking time-consuming. However, your letter is fairly well-written, you sound in dire need, and most importantly, you flatter me, which means you have already learned the first lesson of Manhattan living. Let me help you help us (by bringing us some lunch), kitten.

For starters, let me cut and paste a few easy-breezy tips to living in Manhattan from our New Residents Welcome Pamphlet. Handy things to know: remember that more than two million children worldwide die in excruciating confusion, horror, and pain every year from completely preventable dehydration, so do keep that liter bottle of Naya close as you cab from the office to the gym. Don't forget the three thousand people who die from malaria every day worldwide—only tipple your eight-dollar cocktails in the mosquitoey outdoors when you really need to smoke. We must learn to live in this first world of danger, and sacrifice accordingly.

Why, right now, money from our own taxes is being used to buy the AIDS drug Combivir for a few hundred lucky people in Africa, at what seems to me the outrageous price of one dollar a day per person. That's almost a third of the price of a Starbuck's latte! If only those African people would ease up on their gourmet coffee addictions, it seems to me that they could help themselves with their AIDS problem. But I digress. Anyway, there's a lesson in there for you somewhere.

I have a few questions for you also. You say that you work as a computer programmer. But what do you actually do? I imagine you as a dancer. You sound like one. So we'll talk about your dance career when you arrive at JFK, all fresh-faced and needy in your man-tights.

As you are an artist of movement, I'm a little stunned to hear about your distrust of modernism and art. Does intention mean nothing to you? When you are prancing about the stage, losing yourself in the dim reflection of eyeglasses in the audience, as your sweat spins out in a beautiful spiral, do you not consider the WHY of your flailing girlish arms? When you are learning a new dance, practicing the one true love of your life, do you not seek to find the emotional truth behind your physical exertions? Are you just some fag choreographer's PUPPET, Paul? Indeed. So remember that the only truly commercially viable art has been an art of conceptual intention, wholly apart from any apparent indicator of talent or rigorous practice, since well before you and I were born.

Furthermore, price tags are important, Paul. There is undoubtedly even a price tag attached to your little dance belt, if you know what I mean. Pricing is itself an art, it may in fact be the greatest art of all. (Related: understand stock valuations and you will understand the world, duckie.) Say you made me a pretty day-glo painting (and I'd appreciate it very much, I hope you will). Sadly, as much pleasure as I would get from that painting, I'm afraid the price tag would read WORTHLESS. When I upgrade apartments, as I do every few years, it would undoubtedly end up on a sidewalk outside your quaint little Bowery hostel. (Were you staying at the Gentrification Arms? At the corner of Wanton and Destruction? I love their bar.)

Now: that Sherrie Levine of the knothole pictures to which you refer. First of all, she is represented by an absolute genius and a personal hero of mine, one Miss Paula Cooper. There's a lesson in that, Paul: be represented by a genius. Second lesson: just because we haven't heard of someone, or don't like their latest body of work, does not mean that they aren't important and expensive. Take a good look at the Forbes 400 before you move here.

There will be a quiz, and confusing Daniel, Dirk, and Robert Ziff (of whom I'm sure you've never heard, which does not mean they are not multi-millionaires, see the logic?) at a party will result in your very unballetic party eviction, tiger. There is so much to remember here: in this instance, we must keep track of Sherrie's career. We must remember in which Upper East Side apartment we have seen her photographs. We must pay attention.

Would you like to move to the plastic arts, my little dancer who paints? It can be done, but remember: you will have to attend many many parties and be the funniest or at least most strangely dressed person in the room every weekend, at every dinner and in every bedroom and backroom.

A word or two on income and housing. Admittedly, the job market is a little grim now. Evidently, 1 in 10 working people in the Bronx can't find a job. That's fine—I myself can't find the Bronx. Ha! I kid. You sound childishly unwilling to spend 75% of your income on rent. Perhaps you may be interested in living in Brooklyn (Manhattan's waiting room, it has been called), with something called a "roommate," usually a fellow lost soul with equally bad priorities and fluffy artistic dreams and a complete lack of healthcare, consistent income, hope of retirement, or, really, hope at all.

But that hellish situation will all change over the years in which you live here. For instance, when you meet me, you will only see the Prada and the whitened teeth and the celebrity friends. What you won't see is my past. You won't ever know that when I was very poor and young and new in New York City that, and let me put this delicately, I once was paid $150.00 to insert a very large glass bottle in a Vietnam vet while dressed in a hockey mask and a toga. Don't ever forget that you don't know that, Paul. That 150 bucks lasted me two weeks. Now I take more than that out of the ATM every day. I lose that much at poker every other week. I think there's surely a lesson in that, don't you?

We eagerly await your no-doubt imminent arrival.

Yours truly,

Choire Sicha

President

New York City

PS. You should consider changing your name when you move here. We already have so very many Pauls. Consider something kickier. Or spell it Pawahl. Something impossible to interpret on the page, with a little exotic whiff. Very memorable. And don't look at me in that tone of voice, I was born with this pictogram of a name.

Site: Choire Sicha Dot Com

URL: http://choiresicha.com

Things In The Past Week That Have Brought Me To Uncontrollable, Blubbering Tears

Heather Armstrong

The finely orchestrated piece of crap otherwise known as the finale to "Joe Millionaire."

The look on my dog's face when I took away his bone last night.

The delicate beauty of a Reese's Peanut Butter Cup.

The moment we realized that the bed sheet we bought at Target was too small to fit the mattress for the baby's crib, and the thought of my baby having to sleep on a bed sheetless mattress for the rest of her life.

The amount of money the plumber told us he is going to charge us to move our kitchen sink 24 inches to the right.

The realization that Paris Hilton is someone's daughter.

Almost every sentence on every page of *Under the Banner of Heaven*, by Jon Krakauer.

The fact that my husband can't get a good night's sleep because of my bladder.

The fact that he is always awake to ask me if I'm okay when I return from the bathroom.

Not having enough sugar to complete the recipe for chocolate chip cookies and being unable to make chocolate chip cookies.

Twelve consecutive hours of no chocolate chip cookies in the house.

Having someone at the gym ask me when my baby is due and suddenly realizing, ohmigod, I'm pregnant.

Various segments on NBC's "Today" show specifically engineered to make people in my condition cry, all of them involving the triumph of the human spirit or massive amounts of weight loss.

That one commercial where the guy is painting a wall in his living room and he accidentally backs up and knocks over the can of paint and it goes sprawling all over the wood floors and the Persian rug and he can't do anything but watch it splatter. That poor guy.

Being unable to see the zipper or drawstring on my pants when I pull them up.

Remembering that when I was eight years old I thought I would grow up, have a baby girl and name her either Porsche or Shasta.

A spontaneous bout of heartburn that started over five days ago and has yet to subside.

Seeing a man on television belly flop into a pool of water and thinking that he totally just hurt his baby.

Thinking that there is no way a uterus could fit inside a body that can fit into Victoria's Secret lingerie.

Sending my husband to buy a bulk-sized container of Tucks Medicated Pads.

The sudden death of my step-grandfather, the man who taught me how to play checkers.

Site: Dooce

URL: http://dooce.com

Notes Toward A Constitution For Communal Beach Houses

Choire Sicha

Around the lakes of Minnesota, on the spits and heads of sandbars on the Atlantic, at the rivers of the great Northwest, in the panhandles of all states which panhandle, and in all the islands in the streams, people in their 20s and 30s live in communal temporary arrangements during the short romantic months of summer. While we all at least conceptually understand the basics of living with other people—don't crap with the door open, don't leave your fingernail trimmings on the coffee table—there is a finesse to household arrangement that is often never properly learned.

Time and energy, or their lack, conspire: so frequently, exhausted from our city lives, we rush headlong into these summer arrangements. The results provoke gin and tonic face-splashings in the Hamptons between acquaintances and pantsings between ex-summer-lovers at the Russian River. To hasten the end of these lifestyle disasters, I would like to offer these observed Notes Toward a Constitution for Communal Beach Houses.

One. Each beach house must have a designated area for overly-dramatic personal sharing.

Whether it be a wild shrubbery-enclosed corner of an outdoor deck space, a large claw-footed bathtub, or a Golden-Girls-esque kitchen table, a sacred place must be maintained for snacking and discussions of the heart which will regularly occur during the hours of civil twilight and, of course, after the bars close. Confessions must be put forward ("I too have masturbated in the communal bathroom whilst others waited impatiently outside") and mystic revelations revelated ("I also cried at the last chapter of that awful Frank Herbert book"). These confessions may of course be repeated and work their way into the group joke parlance, but they should never be mocked at the moment of admission. Light another cigarette; practice outward serenity above the scorn roiling inside you.

Two. The Jews and Blacks of the house have control over the way in which the Jews and Blacks are discussed.

It is not appropriate for goyim to use phrases such as "The grocery store has totally Jewed me on the price of these biscuits" without the full approval of the Jew of the house. Likewise, it is not appropriate for white people to give "Shots out to their niggaz." This of course is a matter of common sense for the majority of us. If your house should have neither Jews nor Blacks, you should question your choice of household. If your house is predominately composed of Jews or Blacks, Suggestion Two will be rendered moot, as what would normally sound like anti-Semitic talk will be elevated into a celebration of freedom from Gentiles, and likewise with other groups.

Three. Television is death to community (with certain exceptions).

By its very nature, any television program with commercials is anti-communal. These crimes against household integrity include but are not limited to any show in which matters of dispute are settled before a saucy would-be judge, any show in which neighbors redecorate each other's homes to their mutual chagrin, and anything on the WB. Sporting events are questionable: your mileage may vary from house to house. Golf, for instance, can be strangely soothing of a Sunday afternoon.

Despite their obvious creative flaws, pay-channel dramedies are acceptable communal television watching. Like the plays of Aristophanes, these performances engender understanding of socio-political dynamics such as those that will pass between members of the house. While you yourself may not marry your dippy pregnant vegan girlfriend from Seattle as you break up with your troubled sex-addict girlfriend, someone else in your home certainly will have a similar experience, and it is the wise summer-sharer who is prepared for this sort of crisis.

Four. The Homosexual is in charge of matters relating to taste, plumbing, and salad dressings.

Perhaps your understanding of the role of Homosexuals is limited to observing them be the only housemembers wise enough to bring extra pillows (and what fluffy pillows!) and watching as they secure the window treatments on opening weekend. If that is the case, you have clearly not had the hot water pipings come mysteriously undone, shooting a fountain of steam from the side of your house. You then have never seen the Homosexuals miraculously appear with wrenches, disappear into crawlspaces, and wrestle with stainless hose clamps. Until you have witnessed this, or the equivalent miracle of the tarragon-miso-ginger dressing on watercress, you will not understand the value of the Homosexual in your midst.

Five. It is truly best not to engage in sexual intercourse with fellow housemembers.

As the summer progresses, the strangers among you will become real people. They will also be wearing less and less clothing. In July, that quiet soul reading outside who you've ignored all season will appear on the porch clad only in a speedo. Perhaps, under the influence of Long Island ice tea or the juice of flowers of the forest applied to his eyes by sprites, he will suddenly appear at the door to your bedroom one night. Perhaps you will find yourself alone together on a hot midnight beach as the surf pounds invisibly behind you. You will become yearning. Your lust will surprise you. An imaginary camera will pan the deserted seashore, and in a filmic moment of passion you will rip off your tiny swimsuit and have the best sex of your life.

While it truly is better to regret something you have done than something you haven't, you must believe me that this particular regret will not be unpainful. I am no spokesman for chastity, but I must urge you to resist. The dinner hour will become awkward. Your filthy secret will confess itself to other housemembers. You will become the object of whispers and laughter. Alone again in your bed, you will toss sleeplessly as the mosquito of loneliness whines in your mind. The summer will end and in the winter you will laugh about your moment of vulnerability, but a small part of you will have long since died.

Site: Choire Sicha Dot Com

URL: http://choiresicha.com

Appendix A

Editor's FAQ

We thought you might be interested in how we assembled this book. The following FAQ should answer any questions you may have.

How did you select the best blog content for the book?

A small team of people went from blog to blog, reading thousands and thousands of entries. In fact, we estimate that at least 30,000 blog entries were read in order to narrow the initial selection down to about 170. Not all 170 entries selected could make the final cut due to page count constraints, so we had to cut some entries.

How did you select the entries that made it into the book?

After selecting the initial entries, we assembled them into a special software application written for this project. That content was then sent to a panel of three professional writers who were given instructions to rate the content on how it made them feel. The rating system was from 1 to 5, 5 being the highest.

After the ratings were completed, we averaged the scores, took the highest-rated content, and assembled it for the book. We wanted to ensure that the content wasn't selected by the whims of one or two editors' personal feelings, so we removed ourselves from the process.

Who are the advisors who rated the content?

Pam Ribon: Pamela Ribon is the creator of the hugely successful pamie.com and a writer for TelevisionWithoutPity.com. Her debut novel, *Why Girls are Weird,* landed on Bay Area bestseller lists in its first month. She has since optioned the film rights and is penning the script. She created, directed, and performed in the cult hit *Call Us Crazy: The Anne Heche Monologues,* which drew attention from several major publications, including *People* magazine and The *New York Post.* Pamela has a BFA in acting from the University of Texas at Austin. She currently lives in Los Angeles. She has been known to wear pigtails.

Jack Boulware: Jack Boulware (www.jackboulware.com) is originally from Montana, and he is the author of two nonfiction social history books, *Sex American Style* and *San Francisco Bizarro*. He has received a handful of journalism awards and writes regularly for a wide variety of publications. Stories have taken him to Greenland, Mexico, UK, France, Ukraine, Puerto Rico, Hawaii, and throughout the lower 48 states. In a previous life, he was founding editor of the satirical investigative *Nose* magazine and a columnist for *SF Weekly*. He is co-founder and co-director of the Bay Area's annual Litquake literary festival and is currently working on two new book projects.

Rick Karr: Rick Karr reports on culture and technology for National Public Radio News. He's also a musician, songwriter, and record producer. He's currently writing a book-length history of the technology of popular music. He lives in Brooklyn with his wife, artist and filmmaker Birgit Rathsmann.

What about the content that didn't make the book—can I read it?

Yes. If you visit `http://bestblogs.blogdns.com` you will find links to the content that did not make the final cut. Unfortunately, there just wasn't enough room in the book to include every piece we selected.

A few bloggers in the book have multiple entries. Did they get special consideration?

No. All the bloggers we initially selected had numerous entries up for consideration; however, the final cut of the book is a representation of what the advisors rated as the best content. We took almost everything that scored 3.5 or better. In fact, some content rated high but we had to cut it for other reasons (we were unable to secure permissions, etc.).

Why didn't you announce and ask for submissions?

This isn't a contest or awards show, and we didn't want this to be an audition. If we had asked for submissions, everyone and their uncle would have sent links to content, and it wouldn't have been honest. We wanted content that was written without the perspective that it was auditioning for a spot in a book. And from a management standpoint, we would have been overwhelmed with possibly millions of submissions.

In addition, anything nominated by a public-submission standard tends to be skewed and is not necessarily the best. For example, the blog of a famous writer is not necessarily better than the blog of a virtual unknown, but because the famous writer has a following, she gets more attention.

Did any entries score a perfect 5?

Yes, only one.

This project sounds easy—was it?

It was actually one of the hardest projects we have ever worked on. For one thing, no one has ever collected, edited, or published a book quite like this one. It seemed as though we were confronted by new issues every day. Also, finding the content was, at times, mind numbingly boring. Reading between 100–200 entries a day for months can be a real strain. Some entries were brilliant, but we had to go through 20 or 30 entries to find them. Some blogs have great content but are poorly designed. Some have a great design and are easy to navigate, but the content is weaker. It was like finding a needle in an ever-expanding haystack.

Did you change the blog content at all?

We made some difficult editorial decisions when it came to the content. The goal was simply to present this content as literature. So we made the following changes:

- We didn't want any noise at the beginning of each entry like URL, site name, date, and so on. Each entry starts with the title and author.

- We preserved all the content with no censorship whatsoever.

- We selected content that didn't rely on links to contribute to the content as a whole.

- We corrected spelling and punctuation unless the errors were an integral part of the content.

Some of this content isn't really a blog. What's up with that?

We used a loose definition of what is and isn't a blog. Although some people differentiate between what is a blog, what is journaling, and so on, the masses have already adopted the term "blog" to mean many different things. The line between what is and isn't a blog is now so fine that before too long, differentiating blog and nonblog will be nearly impossible.

We kept to sites we discovered within the blogopshere and looked for individuals who were doing interesting or challenging things with online content. We were looking for people who challenged the future of literature. Each included entry went through intense scrutiny, and we tried to ensure that each entry was true to the nature and feel of the book.

Will there be other books?

We plan on doing a number of books from the blogosphere, including recipes, travel, love/sex/relationships, and more. We also plan to do an anthology each year.

Will you take submissions or nominations for those books?

No. We want to capture good content that isn't *trying* to make it into a book.

Appendix B

Index of Contributors